FREE READER R

As an exclusive and special gift for readers of this book, I have created a private, reader-only page where you can:

- Download valuable resources, including the shook building blocks, bonus trainings, and more.

- Get quick access links to recommended book writing and design resources.

- Get quick access links to recommended book printing resources.

- Get quick access links to recommended book marketing resources.

VISIT:

https://BiteSizedBooks.com/resources

📱 SCAN ME →

BOOKS BY MIKE CAPUZZI

Dream, Inc.

The Ultimate Success Secret (with Dan Kennedy)

3 Steps to Incredible Response

The Entrepreneur's Guide to Marketing with PURLs

Masters of the Mastermind

The Master Mind: Your Ultimate Success Secret

7 Habits of Super Successful Mattress Retailers

High Impact Marketing Manifesto

Just Do This

The Magic of Short Books (Amazon #1 Best Seller)

Main Street Author

WIN WIN WIN

The Magic of Free Books

The 100-Page Book (Amazon #1 Best Seller)

Win Big!

The Magic of Gratitude

The Magic of America

I Love America

PodMatch Host Mastery

PodMatch Guest Mastery

Discover the Power of Using a "Free Book" Marketing
Strategy to Attract New Customers, Clients, or Patients

THE

MAGIC

OF

FREE

BOOKS

A Guide for Business Owners, Entrepreneurs,
and Corporate Leaders on Making Money
By Giving Their Book Away

MIKE CAPUZZI

PUBLISHED BY BITE SIZED BOOKS
A DIVISION OF PERSISTENT MARKETING, INC.

Print ISBN: 979-8-9883098-0-2
eBook ISBN: 979-8-9883098-1-9

051023

BITE SIZED BOOKS

Bite Sized Books publishes direct-response, short, helpful books or shooks™ for business owners,, entrepreneurs, and corporate leaders. Shooks are easy-to-create, quick-to-read, short books. They are designed to be read in about an hour. Bite Sized Books offers a painless process to enable entrepreneurs and business owners to benefit from the authority that comes from being a published author, without the hassle and time commitment normally associated with writing a book. Do you have an idea for a bite sized book you would like us to publish? Visit: https://BiteSizedBooks.com for more details.

CONTENTS

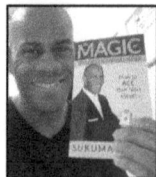

THANK YOU!

Throughout this book you will meet business owners, entrepreneurs, and corporate leaders who have each written a book to differentiate themselves and their respective businesses. Each of these men and women are not concerned about "selling" their books, but instead are focused on getting their books in front of their ideal readers and giving them away for free or almost free.

None of them are "famous" in the typical sense, but each is respected, known, and appreciated by the people they serve.

I want to thank my clients and friends who are featured in this book and acknowledge their sincere efforts to help more people by publishing a helpful book and giving it away.

PART 1

WELCOME

"If there is one book marketing expert who can help you make money by giving away your book, it's Mike Capuzzi. Working with him over the past decade has resulted in a 7-figure payday."

—Jeff Giagnocavo,
Co-owner of Gardner's Mattress & More

WHO SHOULD READ
THIS BOOK?

If you have read any of my other short, helpful books, or shooks™ as I call them, you know I am a huge fan of getting right to the point and minimizing the bloat found in so many business books.

The book you are now reading is <u>very focused,</u> and before you get too far into it, I want to tell you who I wrote it for so that you can make sure it's a smart investment of your time and energy.

● ● ● ●

The Magic of Free Books was written for business owners, entrepreneurs, and corporate leaders who have authored a nonfiction business book designed to share helpful information, promote themselves and their businesses, and plan to give it away for free (or almost free) to targeted readers.

● ● ● ●

Specifically, I am referring to:

- Local business owners, such as dentists, retailers, physicians, lawyers, etc.
- World wide business owners, such as company executives, consultants, and coaches, etc.

These men and women do not focus on writing books as their main "gig" and are not interested in selling their books as the primary way to make money. Instead, they are focused on getting their books into the hands of as many "ideal readers" as possible, typically with a free book offer.

These men and women use their books as conversation starters and then effective follow-up marketing to get readers to become customers (client, patients, etc.).

So, if who I just described sounds like you, then this book was written FOR YOU!

The other important thing to know before you get started is that this is an "idea book" meant to get you thinking about smart ways to market your book. My intention is not to go deep on details, but instead, to present you with a proven set of tactics that my clients and I use to profit from marketing with free books. I don't want to bog you down. Instead, I want to INSPIRE your own free book offer(s).

INTRODUCTION

If you go to Amazon and type "book marketing" in the search bar (using the quotes to get a more focused search), you'll see there is no shortage of books focused on helping authors promote and sell their books. If you then type "free book marketing" (again using quotes) in the search bar, I assume you will see what I just saw when I did this—no specific book results.

This is one of the reasons I decided to write this book. I see a huge void (and opportunity) to help business-focused, non-fiction book authors discover smart ways to give away their books to make sales.

If your goal is to make money by selling your book, then you should be reading one of those other books.

The Magic of Free Books is a marketing book and specifically a direct-marketing book first and foremost. It's about the time-tested strategy of publishing a *strategic, customer-attraction book* (preferably around 100 pages) that solves a big problem for a targeted audience and then offering it as a *lead generation "magnet"* to attract your ideal target readers and compel them to "raise their hand" and request a copy.

The type of free book I suggest you create, besides being short and helpful, follows a specific formula to make the content engaging, interesting, and motivating to take *the next step* in your sales or marketing process with you. These types of books are strategic sales tools designed to inform and motivate. They are NOT meant to be the entire A to Z encyclopedia on your topic.

I've written extensively about the power of these types of short, helpful books and specifically wrote two shooks you should check out—*The 100-Page Book* and *The Magic of Short Books*. You can visit my website for direct links to purchase from your favorite online book seller OR directly from me via a free book offer ☺. Visit:

https://mikecapuzzi.com/author

3 Steps to Turn Free Books into Profits

At a high level, there are only three steps to turn a free book into new customers for your business. If you can consistently and persistently leverage these steps, your book will become a profit machine for your business.

The three steps are:

1. Get your book in front of ideal prospects.
2. Give it away in exchange for contact info.
3. Leverage consistent and effective follow-up.

The Necessary Mind Shift

I urge you to shift your mindset from "selling my book" to being generous with giving your book away and getting as many prospects as possible to want the most valuable marketing asset you've ever produced.

Instead of worrying about how many people are buying your book (like most authors do), shift your focus to generating quality leads (like smart marketers do). Your ultimate goal is to get your book into the hands of as many qualified readers as possible, by making it as irresistible as possible.

I can already hear many of you thinking, *"Whoa, Mike, are you kidding me? My book contains valuable information; therefore, I have to SELL it in order to position its value."*

If this is the way you are thinking, then we are on different pages, because the types of free books I encourage business owners to write are not deep and intense studies on a topic. Yes, they must have useful information, but it's in bite-sized chunks and just enough to help readers move forward. If you have a lengthy or in-depth topic, I highly encourage you to craft several short books instead of one long one.

And while you may encounter some opportunities where you can sell your book, don't let the allure of quick money get in the way of your ultimate goal, which is to attract more ideal customers (clients/ patients/students/members/etc.) as efficiently and effectively as possible.

So, by removing the "stress" of trying to sell your book, I want you to figure out all the different ways you can give your book away to targeted people who would be ideal customers for you and your business.

The Magic of Free Books is also about positioning you differently from your competition and elevating your expert authority on your book's topic. It is not a coincidence that the word *authority* starts with *author*. If you are intrigued by what I call, "the author factor," I highly encourage you to check out my podcast, The Author Factor Podcast, where I interview nonfiction book authors.

https://TheAuthorFactor.com

Types of Free Books

Most free books fall into one of three types (these are in order of my personal preference):

1. Traditional paperback books.
2. eBooks (PDF, Kindle, Flip, etc.).
3. Audio books.

For local business owners, I always encourage using printed books in lieu of digital or audio books. Yes, there is more expense associated with a printed book, but there are many inherent benefits to you and the recipient by providing a paperback book. (Besides, when was the last time you saw anybody autograph a PDF book?)

For business owners who have a national or international market, using digital and audio books can be effective as a starting point, but then quickly offering the print version is smart for so many reasons, including the ability to capture full contact information.

My Challenge to You

Still with me? Then it's time for my first challenge to you. Right now, you are a hunter, hunting for a few free book marketing tactics that resonate with you, make sense for your target readers, and will help you achieve your goals that you can implement now and over the course of the next several months and years. At the very minimum, you want to make sure you create your own Smart Author Toolkit as soon as possible.

My second challenge to you is to make sure you are 100% committed to *consistently* and *persistently* marketing your book and free book offer promotions and opportunities. Over the course of a 30-day month, you should be trying to give away at least 30 copies of your book—one book per day.

To truly profit from the magic of free books, you must be committed to a long-term game that is played over the course of months and years. It is NOT for the business owner who is shortsighted or re-quires a constant shiny, new object to stay motivated. But if you do stay the course, marketing with your free book can be a gamechanger for you and your business (like you are about to see for one company in the next chapter).

Remember, this book is meant to motivate you to take action, not explain every detail of every tactic. Enjoy the ride and make sure you send me your free book offer to check out!

—Mike Capuzzi

Ways to Connect With Me

My websites:

https://MikeCapuzzi.com

https://BiteSizedBooks.com

https://TheAuthorFactor.com

Facebook and LinkedIn:

https://www.facebook.com/michaelmcapuzzi

http://www.linkedin.com/in/mikecapuzzihelps

Mailing address:

470 Boot Rd. #688 Downingtown, PA 19335

> *"For many businesses, including mine, the highest-quality client/customer is initially attracted by a book, and is, by habit, a book buyer and reader. The habit of reading reflects many other attributes that make for a good consumer: intelligence, desire to be informed, ability to process complex information, respect for authoritative sources, and thoughtful rather than impulsive decision making."*

—Dan Kennedy

A HISTORY OF
THE FREE BOOK OFFER

I love studying the history of business and specifically marketing. So, before we jump into the specific free book marketing tactics, I want to share a history lesson, so you have a deeper understanding and appreciation of just how long the free book offer has been around.

Here is a unique exercise to prove my point:

1. Go to https://books.google.com and type in "free book offer" with the quotes and hit the search button.

2. Click on the TOOLS button.

3. Click on the down arrow next to ANY TIME and select 19th CENTURY.

4. Click on the SORTED BY RELEVANCE down arrow and choose SORTED BY DATE.

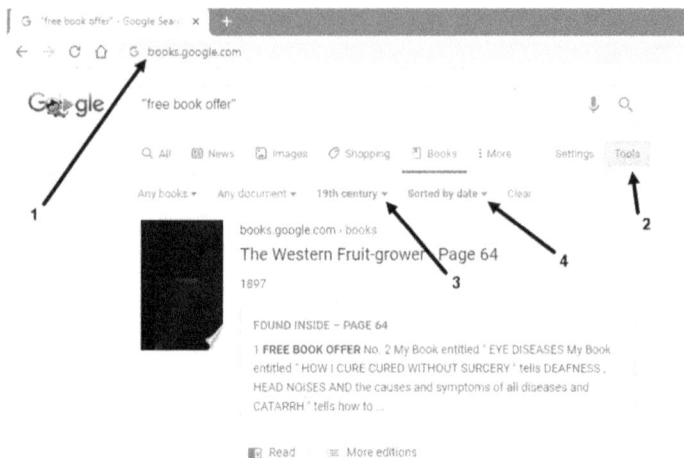

If you then go to the next page (my search only has two pages of results), you will see that the very first instance where you can actually read the publication is from 1892 in *The Phrenological Journal and Science of Health.* Here is a screenshot of it.

If you are a history geek, and you start searching in the early 1900's, you will see a flood of free book offers in a variety of publications.

One of the classic and longest-running free book offers comes from Ostermoor, a mattress manufacturing company that was founded in 1853 and is still in business today. During my research, I found an Ostermoor print ad from 1903, which features a free book offer. My guess is there are earlier ads, but this one is the oldest I could find.

This ad and many others that followed for the next several decades offered a free copy of their book, *The Test of Time.*

Ostermoor offered their free book for decades in the early- and mid-20th century. Interestingly, you can buy a reproduction of *The Test of Time* on Amazon and see even more vintage ads at:

https://OstermoorMattress.com/test-of-time

There are countless examples of both well-known and lesser-known brands leveraging a free book marketing strategy since 1903, including fitness products and even garden equipment.

If a mattress company can successfully use a free book offer for decades, what do you think you can do? The free book offer can be one of the most strategic and profitable marketing strategies you can leverage in your business, if you remember these three keys...

The Keys to Using a Free Book Strategy

There are three critical things all book authors must do in order to create profitable results from their free book marketing efforts:

1. You must be <u>consistent</u> and <u>persistent</u> in your use of each tactic you decide to implement. Make sure you have a long-term vision and stay the course. Marketing with a free book is a long-term game.

2. You must <u>evaluate</u> and <u>adjust</u> your efforts over time. I would not recommend a "set and forget" strategy, unless you are getting great results.

3. Regardless of how good your free book marketing is, it will not provide optimal results, unless you have <u>effective</u> and <u>quality follow-up marketing</u> in place. Make sure your entire team understands this and does their best job possible.

If there is one big mistake I have seen book authors make repeatedly, it's this: after the initial excitement of publishing the book, life, business, and other things get in the way of using it–every day. To combat this, remember why you wrote it and the fact that unless people know about it, you will not be able to help them with it.

*Make sure you take advantage
of all the valuable resources you get
for free as a reader of this book!*

My Private Shook Reader Resources Page

MY RESOURCES:

- Read *The Magic of Working Together*
- My shooks on Amazon
- My shooks on my website
- The Author Factor Podcast
- My High-Impact Marketing Tips
- My Shook Building Blocks
- My "Special Sauce" newsletter issue

MY TRAININGS

- Download my *100-Page Book Blueprint* training (videos)
- Download my *100-Page Book Blueprint* training (slides)
- Download my *100-Page Book Blueprint* training (blocks)
- Download my Big Idea training
- Download my WOW! Kit training.

RECOMMENDED RESOURCES

- FlipBuilder.com
- PodMatch (my podcasting "secret weapon")

https://BiteSizedBooks.com/resources

PART 2

THE SMART AUTHOR TOOLKIT

> *"I urge you to affix your mind to the thought process of being generous with giving your book away and getting as many prospects as possible to hold the most valuable marketing asset you've ever produced in their hands."*

**—Bob Regnerus,
Co-Founder of Feedstories.com**

THE SMART AUTHOR TOOLKIT

In this section, I am focusing on the fundamental book marketing assets I believe EVERY business owner, entrepreneur, and corporate leader who has written a non-fiction, business-oriented book should leverage.

By developing your own Smart Author Toolkit, you will have a *go-to* set of assets you can use for the variety of marketing tactics I share in the rest of this book.

Trust me, the time, effort, and money invested in creating this toolkit will pay for itself over and over again for the next several years. I challenge you to leverage as many of these as possible in your book marketing efforts.

נשיא המדינה

ירושלים, י' בתמוז תשע"ד
08 ביולי 2014

לכבוד
ערן שטרן, מנכ"ל
<u>"יוצא מהכלל" אימון להצלחה</u>

ערן היקר,

ברצוני להודות לך על ספרך "**להנשים**" אשר הענקת לי.

מבין דפי הספר עולים עצות ורעיונות מעניינים, מסקרנים ומעוררי מחשבה, הנטועים באמונה ברוחו האופטימית והחיונית של האדם.

הפוטנציאל הטמון באדם פנימה, בכל אדם, הוא כה גדול, שלעיתים אין אנו מודעים למלוא עומקו. ספרך נועד לסייע בגילוי והעצמת מודעות זו - להעז, לשנות ולהגשים.

ראה ברכה בספרך וביוזמותיך.

יישר כוח,

שמעון פרס

Thank-you Letter From President Shimon Peres

ALWAYS CARRY BOOKS WITH YOU

A super easy way to get your book in the hands of ideal readers is to simply carry a few copies with you everywhere you go. You never know who you may meet at an event, on an airplane, or simply when you are out and about. I always carry a few copies of my books with me wherever I go, and I even have a small container of them in my car—just in case.

Trust me, if you do this consistently, unique opportunities will present themselves, which will allow you to get your book in front of ideal prospects or even a V.I.P. You never know who you might bump into during a normal day.

This happened to Eran Stern, who shared on my podcast one of the most powerful examples of why it's important to carry your book with you. By having his book with him, he was able to give a copy to the President of Israel, who then sent him a thank-you letter (shown on previous page). This is worth listening to:

https://AuthorFactor.com/eran-stern

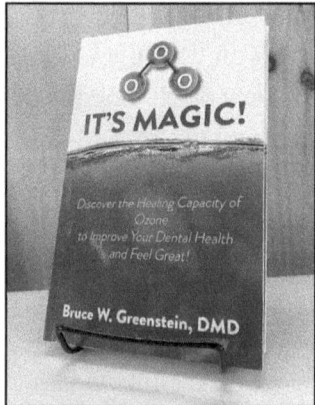

Book Display Examples

DISPLAY YOUR BOOKS

Displaying your book in places where your ideal targeted readers can see it is a smart and effective strategy you should use. You can either display your book in your own locations or the locations of what I call "strategic partners."

Over the years, I have used a variety of inexpensive but effective displays for my own books and for my clients' books. I've even gone as far as working with a local metal fabricator and a local woodworker to custom create my own book displays (see the top two display on the previous page). You can find nice displays online at Amazon, including:

- Wire easel displays.
- Acrylic displays.
- Wooden displays.

Whichever style you decide to use, just make sure you are placing them in highly visible locations. I list a number of recommendations on your reader resource page.

Yours Tribally,

Nigel Moore 🤓
Leader of <u>The Tech Tribe</u>
Author of <u>Package Price Profit</u>

p.s. Connect with me on <u>Facebook</u> & <u>LinkedIn</u>

Author Signature Examples From Nigel Moore

CREATE AN
AUTHOR SIGNATURE

Most business owners never publish a real book, which automatically puts you in a valuable and prestigious club—the "Author's Club."

This is an extremely important point of distinction for you and your business, and you MUST embrace it and fully leverage it in order to leverage your book(s) fully.

One of the easiest things you can do is to make sure you add the title "Author of <YOUR BOOK TITLE>" to your email signature, business cards, biography, social media descriptions, etc. The more places you can feature your book and you as the author of it, the better your chances for getting the right people to see it and want it.

You should be able to create a simple email signature like my client, Nigel Moore, did when he published *Package Price Profit*. If you do not know how to do this, Google "email signature generator" and you will find a number of resources to help.

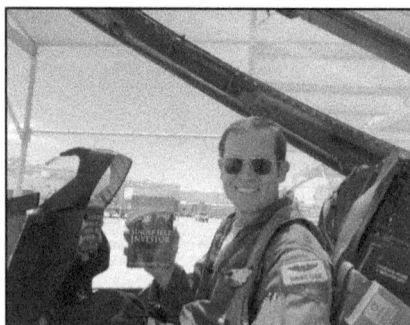

Author Photo Examples From Dominic Teich

CREATE A BOOK
AUTHOR PHOTO KIT

The first important type of graphic to have in your Smart Author Toolkit is a variety of photographs of you with your book. This is one of the most eye-catching and important types of photos to have and use.

Take a few formal ones in business attire and in front of appropriate backgrounds and take a few casual ones in appropriate settings. Just make sure your book is visible and you are not covering the title or your name with your hand.

If your book has a certain target audience or theme, make sure you take appropriate photos like my client, Dom Teich, did when he posed in front of his F-16 jet. Dom is a fighter pilot and wrote a book for pilots, so capturing this type of photo was critical.

If you are doing paid social media advertising, use a photo of you holding your book instead of a graphic of the book by itself. Author photos are more eye-catching as people are scrolling through their feed.

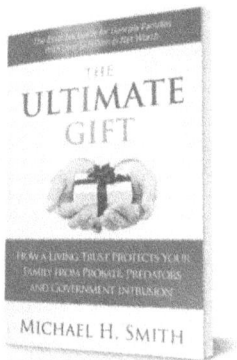

Cover Image Examples From Michael Smith

CREATE A BOOK
COVER IMAGE KIT

Once your book cover is finalized, you should have your designer create a set of print-ready 3D cover images for your use in both your online and offline marketing. They should be able to do this for you very easily. If not, Google "3D book covers" for a number of resources.

Creating high-resolution 3D cover images of your book enables you to have professional-quality graphics for use on signs, printed business collateral, print ads, and social media. Just make sure when they are created, they are high resolution and have transparent backgrounds so you can use them on any type of background. You will see many examples in this book of how we used my 3D book covers and my clients' 3D covers.

Personally, I use the 3D cover images of my various books daily, so it's important you get your own set of images for your own consistent use.

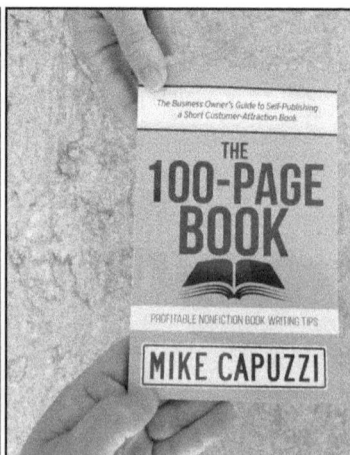

Book Photo Examples From My Kit

CREATE A BOOK
PHOTO KIT

The third type of "must-have" graphics for your book-marketing efforts are eye-catching photographs of your printed book. These types of photos are focused on the book only, and once you have your printed book, I recommend you take some nice photos of it, including these shots:

- Hand holding your book.

- Handing your book to another person.

- Book standing up.

- Open book on surface.

- Book in your office, store, place of business.

Take both close-up photos and distant shot photos (depending on the background). Personally, I am a big fan of taking photos on rustic wood platforms, which I had specifically made for the purpose of book photos.

Use these photos in all your offline and online marketing efforts.

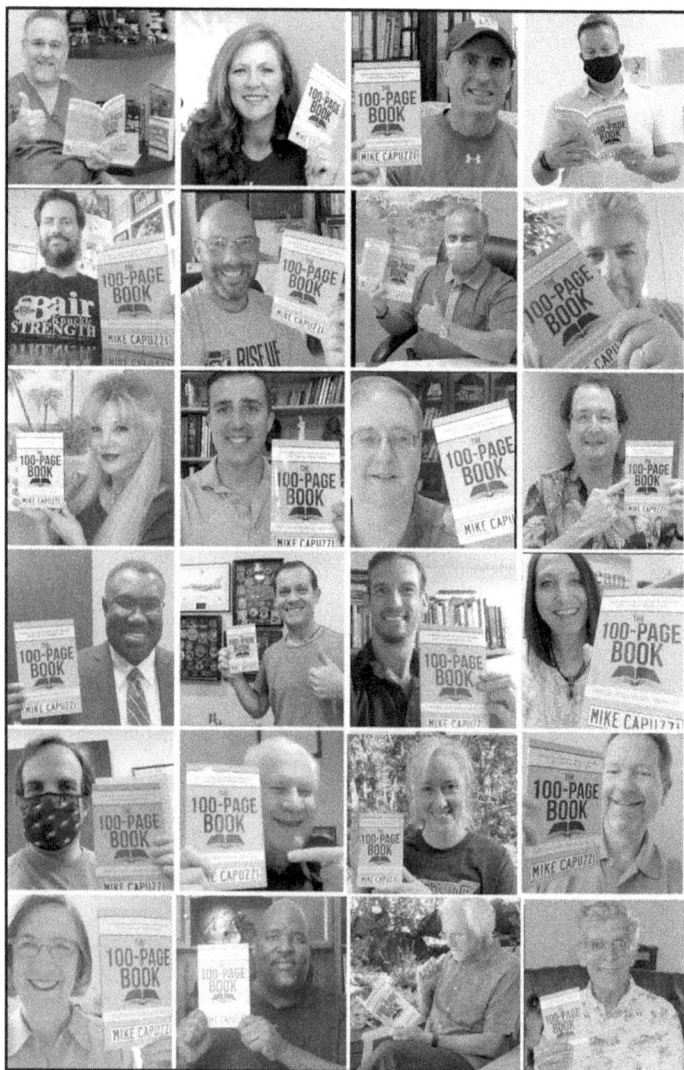

Book Reader Photo Examples From My Kit

CREATE A BOOK
READER PHOTO KIT

The last type of graphics I highly recommend you create are book reader photos. If you can get your readers to send you photographs of them reading your book, they can be quite effective images to motivate others to get a copy too.

Much like collecting book testimonials, you need a specific and consistent strategy to ask readers to send in photos. Typically, a social media contest or some sort of "gift in return for a photo" effort is required to get readers to send in photos.

When I published *The 100-Page Book*, I sent out 50 pre-release copies to people who I knew and asked them for both a testimonial and a photograph of them with the book. About half responded, but it was enough to create an impressive collection of both written testimonials and photos, which I was able to leverage during the book launch.

If you offer your book in your place of business, you could easily (and quickly) ask for a photo of the person with your book. In my experience, most people will happily oblige.

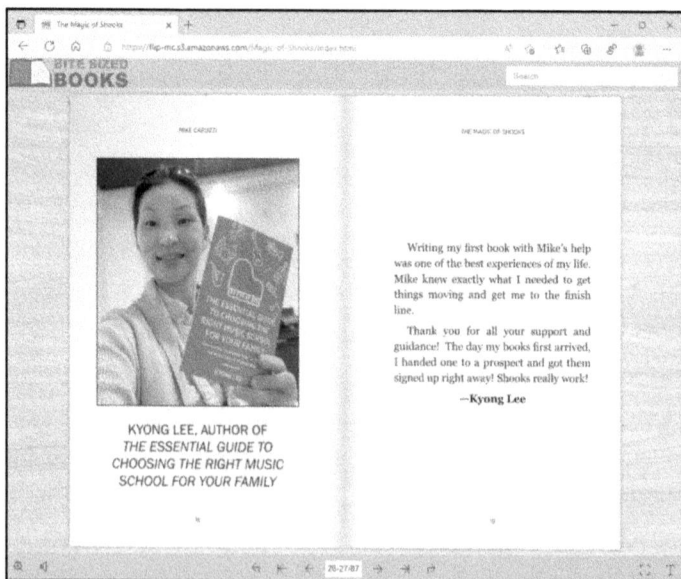

Book Reader Testimonial Examples From My Kit

CREATE A BOOK
READER TESTIMONIAL KIT

Asking for and sharing testimonials about your book is a smart "social proof" strategy and helps you build a valuable collection of feedback from real-world readers.

There are many ways to ask readers for book testimonials—both online and offline. The key is to <u>consistently ask</u>. Start with the cover letter you include when you send a copy in the mail, and then use email follow-up to remind the reader how important book testimonials are for your business. Realize only a small handful of readers will actually take the time to do this, so do not get frustrated if you only get a few. You can host a contest or offer a thank -you gift to generate more testimonials.

Once you start getting them, then you must use them in the marketing and promotion of your book. Wherever you offer your book, include a few testimonials. I use testimonials on my website, and I have even created a "Flip" book, *The Magic of Working Together*, to send to prospects. Check it out at:

https://BiteSizedBooks.com/authors

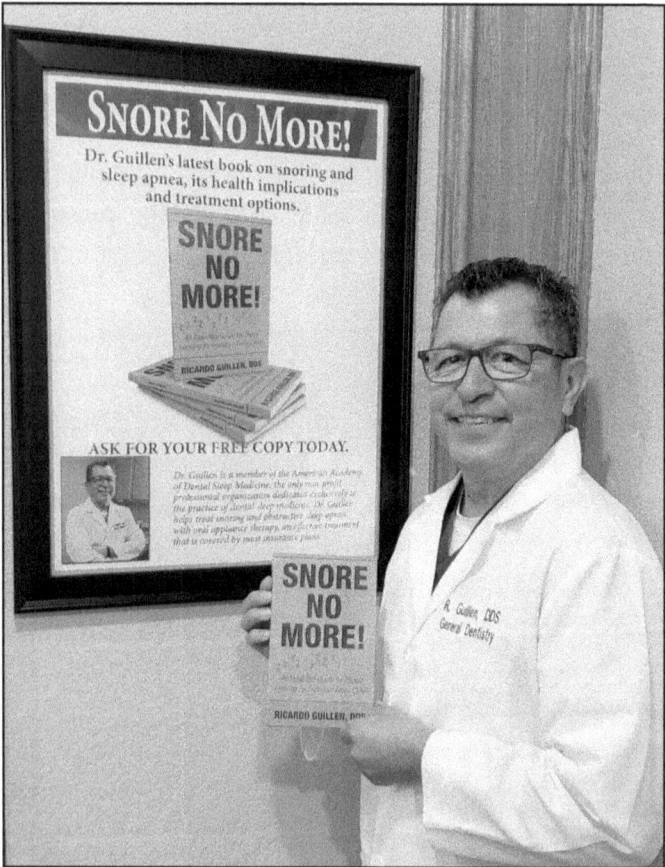

Book Poster Example From Dr. Ricardo Guillen

CREATE BOOK POSTERS & SIGNS

Featuring your book as a poster, office/store wall art, or signage is a unique and effective way to showcase your book. You can also use this type of wall art at events and with strategic partners.

My client, Dr. Ricardo Guillen, did a great job leveraging this tactic when he created several poster-size prints that he framed and placed throughout his dental practice office. As you can see, Dr. Guillen used the 3D cover images we created for him to create his posters.

Dr. Guillen has also placed copies of his book in his waiting room and other strategic areas in his office. All of this adds up to increased opportunities for visitors and patients to pick up a copy for themselves or a family member or friend.

Your place of business and other physical places where your ideal readers can be found are an important type of marketing "media" that you should take advantage of.

FOSTERWEBMARKETING.COM

Tom Foster
Founder | CEO
TomFoster@FosterWebMarketing.com
(866) 227-6550

10555 Main St, Suite 470A
Fairfax, VA 22030

FWMANALYSIS.COM

5 Essential Rules for Crafting Online
Content to Connect With Your Perfect
Clients, Patients or Customers

THE
KILLER CONTENT
BLUEPRINT

ATTRACT   CONVERT   RETAIN

TOM FOSTER

Learn how to master the art of
online content marketing in
The Killer Content Blueprint.

Author Card From Tom Foster

CREATE A BOOK AUTHOR CARD

Creating a book-specific author card is a useful tool to carry with you and insert in printed book copies you give out. They also make nice little bookmarks for your readers.

Sized like a normal business card, an author card should be a double-sided card that includes your contact information on the front side and your book information on the second side. Smart things to include on the book-specific side are:

- Your book's website or the website where someone can get your book.

- An image or photo of your book.

- A helpful and interesting "one-liner" about your book or how you serve your customers.

- A V.I.P. testimonial about your book.

- The series' covers (if you have a series of books).

- Social media contact information.

FOSTER WEB MARKETING

FIND OUT WHAT'S HELPING AND WHAT'S HURTING YOUR ONLINE PRESENCE AT FWMANALYSIS.COM

TWO-MINUTE WARNING:

Winning the Game of Hair Loss

Former NFL player and acclaimed hair restoration surgeon, John Frank M.D., has helped thousands of men reclaim confidence and self-esteem through his cutting edge men's hair restoration solutions.

Step # 1 is to schedule your own Frank & Honest Hair Consultation today!

Scan to schedule:

John Frank, M.D.
833-860-1312
www.JohnFrankMD.com

My Promise to You:

I am committed to providing you with the best possible care and results. I understand the emotional impact that hair loss has, and I am dedicated to helping my patients regain their confidence and self-esteem. I promise to provide a personalized treatment plan tailored to your unique needs and goals. I am sincerely interested in seeing my patients' hair loss reversed, and I work tirelessly to achieve that result. My goal is not just to provide a hair transplant but to ensure that you achieve a natural-looking and long-lasting result that meets your expectations.

—Dr. John Frank

Book-Specific Bookmarker Examples

CREATE A BOOKMARKER

A book-specific bookmarker is a useful and super-inexpensive way to promote your book and drive readers to do the next thing you want them to do after reading your book. Most readers will appreciate and use the bookmarker, which means it gives you, the opportunity to keep your message in front of them.

Here are some things you should consider including in your bookmarker design:

- Quality paper stock (I like 14 pt. gloss).

- Use both sides.

- Your author photo.

- Your book image.

- Your book's "big idea."

- A specific message or instruction for book readers on what to do next.

- Specific ways to take "the next step" (e.g., QR code, URL link, phone #).

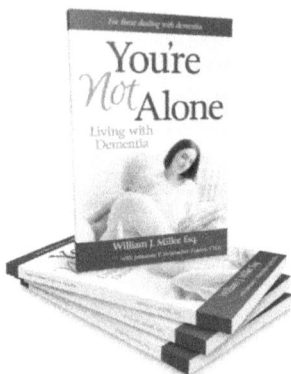

FREE BOOK OFFER!

My new book is written for families dealing with dementia.

You're *Not* Alone

Living with Dementia

William J. Miller Esq.

Please take this card with you.

RE'S HOW TO GET A FREE COPY OF MY BOOK...

nk you for your interest in getting a free copy of our book, *You're Not Alone: Living with Dementia.*

My book is designed to be read in about an hour or two and provides essential clear and simple advice, guidance and tips.

Each chapter in this concise book provides important information and resources to protect loved ones and maintain independence for as long as possible.

You're Not Alone: Living with Dementia retails for $9.95, but for a limited time you can get the paper-back version for FREE (just pay shipping & handling). There is no obligation and you can read it in the privacy and comfort of your home.

To get your copy of my book, please call:

256-241-6794

Bill Miller

www.MillerEstateandElderLaw.com

MILLER
ESTATE AND ELDER LAW

Book Promo Card From Bill Miller

CREATE A BOOK PROMO CARD

A book "promo card" is a specialized type of postcard/flyer that is used whenever you want to display your book in places where your ideal readers will see it (like in other local businesses—see page 107). Think of it as a "take away with you" brochure like what you see in hotel lobby displays featuring local places of interest, restaurants, etc.

A book promo card gives you an inexpensive way to "display" your book and allow people to take the card with them to remind them to get your book. You can place them in inexpensive, acrylic display cases, sized to fit your promo card. Our cards are sized at 5.5" x 8.5" and fit nicely into the 5.5" wide brochure holders that I recommend in your reader resources page. Keep these in mind as you design it:

- Use the power of a FREE BOOK OFFER as your headline.

- Include an attention-grabbing book graphic.

- Give multiple ways for people to get it (URL, phone, QR code).

Book Mailer Kit Example From Dr. John Frank

CREATE A BOOK MAILER KIT

There are two types of "book mailer" packages I think every author should be using to send out a printed copy of his or her book. The first is a simple but effective book mailer, and the second is a WOW! Kit mailer. In cases where you want a simple and cost-effective way to mail your book, I recommend sending your book in a small, padded envelope, which not only stands out but also protects your book. You can check out my recommended resources on the reader resources page.

We created a great-looking and effective book mailer kit for my client, Dr. John Frank, which consisted of:

- Bright orange padded envelope.

- His short, helpful book.

- A cover letter "postcard."

- A bookmarker (with QR code to his primary call-to-action).

- An autographed photo of him during his NFL days.

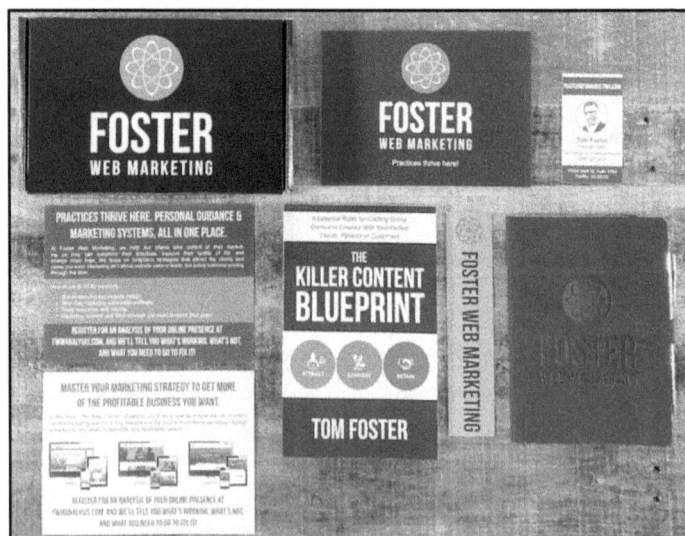

WOW! Kit Example From Tom Foster

CREATE A BOOK WOW! KIT

Building a WOW! Kit around your book is a smart strategy and a unique service we offer to our publishing clients. I send WOW! Kits to new clients, suitable prospects, podcast hosts, and joint-venture prospects. My client, Tom Foster, created a powerful WOW! Kit which includes:

- A custom-printed box.
- A thank-you card.
- An author card.
- A postcard-sized "brochure".
- A bookmarker.
- A custom-engraved pen.
- A JournalBook™.

I created a powerful 25-minute "mini training" that goes into more detail on how to build your own WOW! Kit. Get it at:

https://BiteSizedBooks.com/resources

NATE LIND
Author of *Maximum Exit*

HOW I HELP OTHERS: One afternoon hiking with my kids caused a gut wrenching realization that inspired me to sell my first business and focus more on my health, my family and other passions. Entrepreneurs that read *Rich Dad Poor Dad* or *The Four Hour Work Week* want financial freedom. Many find themselves working harder than ever and without the financial freedom they wanted. That was me. Burnt out, stressed out, working more, and making less as an entrepreneur than I would have if I've just stayed a vice president at Bank of America. My story will help your audience reconnect with WHY they became entrepreneurs and show them the BEST way to reach it. I'm fighting for entrepreneurs to use their businesses to exit the rat race. I fight against businesses that isolate owners from their families and new passions. I've had the privilege of selling my and my client's companies at wild multiples. The process is repeatable and within reach. Selling their company is the BEST way for entrepreneurs to reconnect with their families, and explore new passions.

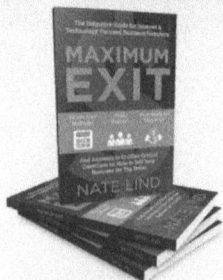

SUGGESTED INTRODUCTION:

Nate Lind, is an American entrepreneur, triathlete, author and business broker. Reading Rich Dad Poor Dad inspired Lind to dream of financial freedom and passive income. He exited his first company in 2016, which was an e-commerce technology to a shopping cart platform. Lind learned that selling a company and using the proceeds to buy passive income was far easier than trying to run it passively.

Nate sells companies like Realtors sell homes. He is a business broker at Website Closers, the largest marketplace of $1 million to $150 million dollar Internet, Technology and E-commerce businesses. There are 167,000 buyers looking at 103 client businesses for sale right now. This year they will sell over 300 companies to their private network.

INTERVIEW TOPIC IDEAS:

- The Life Changing Benefits of Selling Your Business for Top Dollar
- The BEST Way Entrepreneurs Can Build Passive Income
- Selling Your Company Yourself vs. Working with an Intermediary
- How To Sell Your Business for Top Dollar
- How To Figure Out What Your Business Is Worth

INTERVIEW QUESTION IDEAS:

1. *What mistakes do entrepreneurs make when it comes to selling their business?*
2. *What is my company worth? How is that determined?*
3. *When's the best time to sell?*
4. *What are the deal structures like? (cash vs. earnout)*
5. *Aren't we in a recession? What is the market demand for companies like mine?*
6. *How can I increase the value?*
7. *What can decrease the value?*
8. *What factors tend to kill deals?*

BRAND NEW BOOK!

Maximum Exit was written for busy company owners and burnout founders who want to achieve the maximum selling price for their business. Designed to be read in about an hour, Maximum Exit shares Nate's formula to achieve your own Maximum Exit!

CONNECT WITH NATE:

- nate@websiteclosers.net
- facebook.com/findnate
- linkedin.com/in/natelind
- 797-209-9222

Podcast One Sheet Example From Nate Lind

CREATE A BOOK AUTHOR ONE SHEET

The Author One-Sheet is a strategic one-page document that you send to podcast/event hosts, along with your pitch email. Your one-sheet is an attractively designed and compelling collection of "reasons why" you would be a suitable guest and how your expertise will be of interest and help to the host's listeners/attendees. I like to include my one-sheet in my book's media kit.

Here are some things to include in your one-sheet:

- Your key focus on how you help others.
- Your short business bio.
- Why you would be a good guest.
- What you can talk about and share.
- Information about your specific book.
- Suggested questions the host can ask you.
- Suggested topics you can speak about.
- The various ways people can connect with you.

Nate Lind Recording His Audio Book

CREATE AN AUDIO BOOK

The popularity of audio books is growing, and turning your book into an audio book could be a smart way to leverage it. There are several paths you can take to get your audio book completed:

1. Record your book yourself using your own recording equipment. While this is the most cost-effective, unless you have high-quality equipment and a quiet place to record, audio quality may suffer.

2. Record your book yourself in a professional recording studio and have an audio pro edit it. This can cost several hundred to several thousand dollars.

3. Hire a professional voice-over artist to record it and have an audio pro edit it. This can cost several hundred to several thousand dollars but is painless for you.

4. Look at A.I. (artificial intelligence) options for creating high-quality, multiple-language versions very quickly.

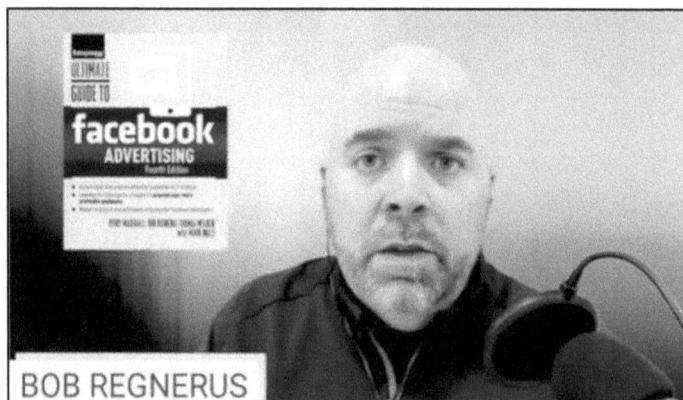

Book Promo Videos From Bob Regnerus

CREATE A BOOK VIDEO PROMOTION

Creating a promotional book video to announce the debut of your book is an effective and engaging way to debut your book. The strategic use of quality video, graphics, customer or reader testimonials, and music put together in a short (less than five minute video) is a powerful addition to your Smart Author Toolkit. Here's an outline for your video:

- Open with captivating music and graphics.
- Introduce yourself as the book author and who your book was written for.
- Describe why it's important for your target reader to get the book.
- Describe the outcome your target reader will get after they read the book.
- Share customer/reader testimonials.
- Share how to get a copy of your book.

You can go the do-it-yourself route or work with a professional digital marketing expert, like my friend Bob Regnerus, co-founder of Feedstories.com.

Press Release Example From Dr. John Frank

CREATE A BOOK PRESS RELEASE

Announcing the debut of your book via a local (or in some cases, national) press release is a powerful way to build buzz around a new book release and generate media attention. Your release should provide a brief summary of the book, highlight its key features and benefits, and offer quotes or endorsements from relevant experts or influencers.

In addition to generating media coverage, a press release can also be used as a marketing tool on social media and other online platforms. By sharing the release on your website and social media channels, you can generate excitement around your new book.

For local business owners who are now authors, this can be a super smart way to get local media coverage for free. Of course, you have to follow effective press release writing tactics and media strategies to make all this happen, but it can definitely happen. If you do not have a press release writing and distribution partner, check out this book's free resources for my personal recommendation.

https://AiForBookAuthors.com

LEVERAGE ARTIFICIAL INTELLIGENCE BOOK MARKETING AUTOMATION

I would be remiss to not mention artificial intelligence (AI) in a marketing-focused book published in 2023. Truth be told, I am personally only a few months into experimenting with AI and in one word I am AMAZED at the opportunities AI offers book authors. Fortunately, I am working with the team of AI-focused professionals at BehaviorSales.com to create an AI-based framework for book authors to leverage in four distinct ways:

1. Creating your own AI "persona" that has learned your specific "voice", methods, and solutions based upon your book(s), articles, videos, interviews, etc., so that all future content generated sounds like you.

2. Book-specific chatbots (imagine having an interactive bot on your website that can help prospects answer their own questions).

3. Book launch content and automation.

4. Ongoing book promotion automation.

For more details scan the QR code on page 58.

PART 3

SOCIAL SHARING TACTICS

"Free books truly are magic. There's simply no better way to get your audience's attention and educate them about your offering than through free books. We've had great success marketing our estate planning legal services through our first free book. In fact, it's worked so well that we're planning to do a second one."

—Michael H. Smith, Esq.
Co-Founder at Smith Barid, LLC

SOCIAL SHARING TACTICS

In this section I am going to focus on what I call "social sharing tactics." These tactics focus on a variety of ways you can get your book in front of your ideal readers by simply sharing it in many different ways.

As you read through this section, I challenge you to identify the social sharing tactics you can and should start using immediately.

My Book Bonus Offer

GIVE YOUR BOOK AWAY AS A BONUS IN ANOTHER BOOK

Here's an interesting bit of trivia. The book you are now reading was initially a special book I created to be used as a "bonus book" in my other books as a lead magnet. I wrote the original version of this book in 2020 and used it as a reader gift in both *The 100-Page Book* and *The Magic of Short Books* for about a year. During that period, several hundred readers opted-in and requested this book. You can still see the funnel at

https://MarketingWithFreeBooks.com

In order to make this an exclusive offer, *The Magic of Free Books* was not available anywhere else but my funnel, and I used my book printer to print the books, which we mailed out personally.

Whether you create a special book (like I did) or use one of your older books, this is a powerful tactic to encourage your readers to take action and connect with you.

Always dreamed about writing that book? Well, here's your chance! Grab these FREE books, get enormous value, and finally become the author you always wanted to be!

Get FREE instant access to all of them for a limited time only as part of this promotion to give back and change the world

~~These Books Will Disappear at Midnight November 18th~~

These awesome books are available for just a little more time! Take action and grab them NOW!

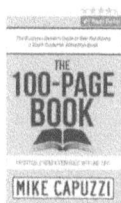

| 02 | 11 | 31 | 55 |
| DAYS | HOURS | MINUTES | SECONDS |

The 100-Page Book

Relaunch Your Life

Trickle Down Mindset

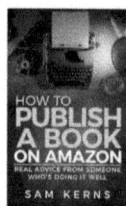

How to Publish a Book on Amazon in 2020

My Book Included in a Book Promotion

GIVE YOUR BOOK AWAY AS A BONUS IN OTHER PEOPLES' PROMOTIONS

This is sort of a no-brainer tactic, but one I even forget to do, which is to offer your book as a bonus for your other marketing and advertising promotions or for other people's promotions.

For example, if you host events for prospects, you can offer your book as a bonus when they register for your event. I have seen this used successfully to add value to both in-person and virtual events.

Another opportunity is to use your book as a bonus in another business owner's promotion. I recently did this with a gentleman who hosts a free book giveaway, where a number of authors include their book, and then they all promote to their lists. In return, I got the contact information for all the people who downloaded my free book. The net result was 1,233 new people who downloaded my book.

The bottom line is your book is a valuable asset, and using it as a bonus, follow-up incentive, or gift are just more smart ways to leverage your book.

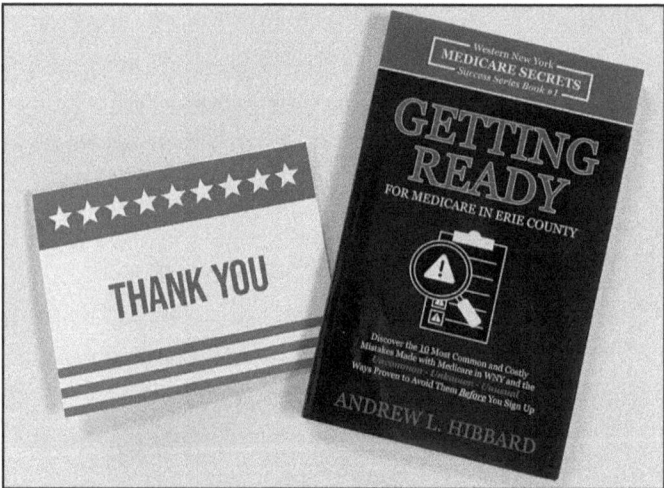

Thank-you Gift Example from Andrew Hibbard

GIVE YOUR BOOK AWAY
AS A THANK-YOU GIFT

Your book is a valuable gift that readers can enjoy. Unlike some other thank-you gifts, such as discounts, promotional gifts, or food items, a book is a product that readers can use and appreciate for years to come. Here are a few other reasons I like to use my books as thank-you gifts:

Giving away your book as a gift helps to build relationships with readers. By providing a valuable gift, you can build trust with your audience, which can lead to increased loyalty and support.

When readers receive a book as a thank-you gift, they may be more likely to share their experience with others, leading to increased word-of-mouth marketing and potential new fans for you.

Finally, giving away a book as a thank-you gift can be a cost-effective way to show appreciation and build relationships with readers. While some other gifts may require a significant investment or re-sources, giving away a book is a low-cost strategy that can yield significant returns in terms of building loyalty and generating buzz and business.

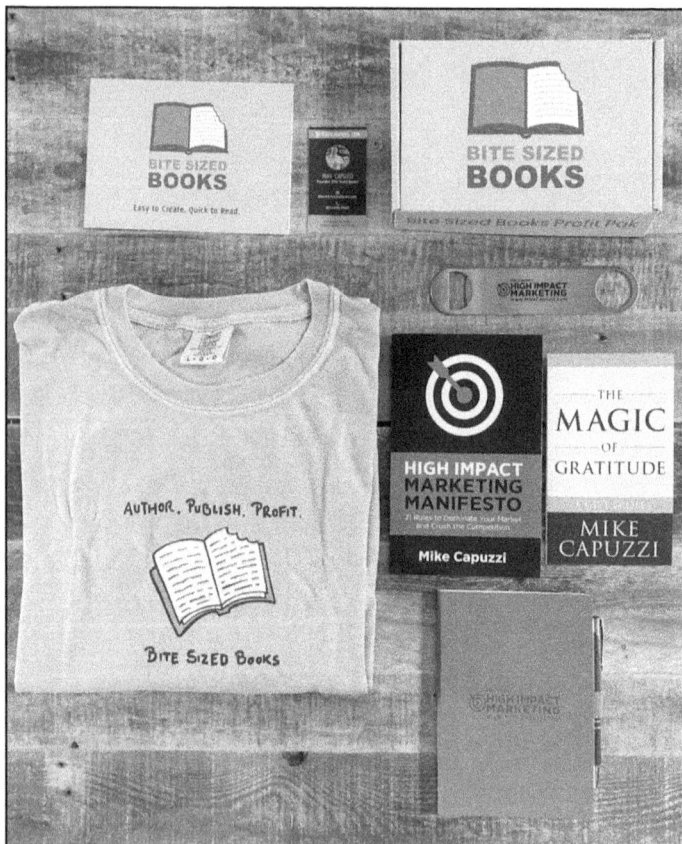

My New Client Welcome Gift

GIVE YOUR BOOK AWAY AS PART OF A NEW CUSTOMER WELCOME GIFT

Depending on your business, creating a "New Customer" (Client/Patient/Student) Welcome Gift is a powerful (and often unexpected) way to showcase how you and your business are different. Including your book, a different book you have authored, or even a specifically designed "gift book" plus other useful and fun gifts is smart.

I send my new clients a welcome gift when they join one of my publishing programs, packaged up into one of our custom Bite Sized Books boxes. Here is what I typically include:

- Handwritten thank-you card.
- Author card.
- Customized bottle opener.
- Bite Sized Books T-shirt.
- *High Impact Marketing Manifesto*.
- *The Magic of Gratitude* (gift book).
- Custom imprinted JournalBook™ and pen set.

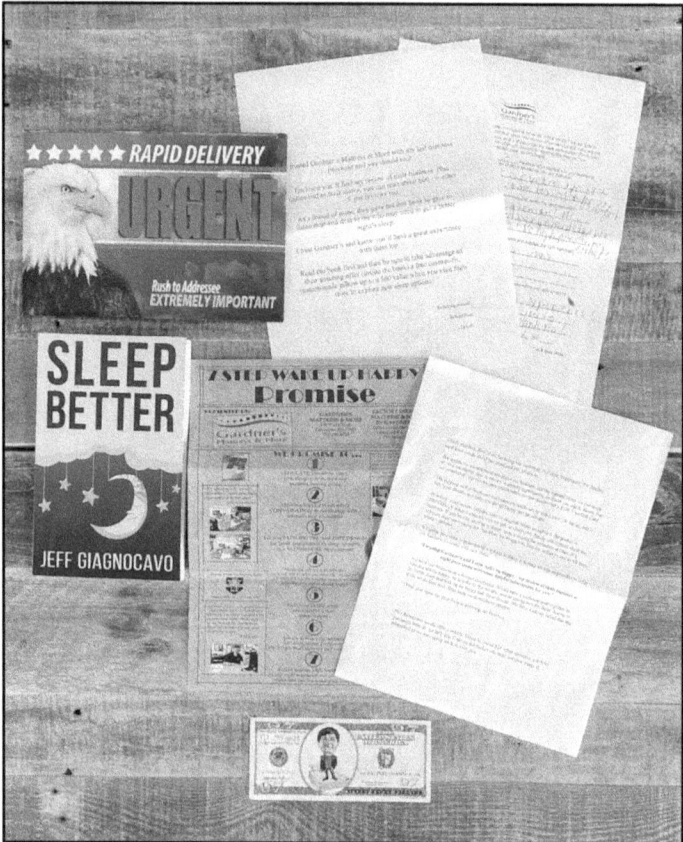

Referral Kit Example From Jeff Giagnocavo

GIVE YOUR BOOK AWAY AS PART OF A REFERRAL PROGRAM

If you are a local business owner, you can tap into the power of giving away your book via other people's networks—specifically your employees' and customers' spheres of influence. This can be a very effective way to get your book in the hands of ideal readers.

Give copies of your book to employees and encourage them to give it to people they know who can benefit from what you offer. Create a monthly contest for employees and award prizes for the team members who generate the most new business. Remind them that helping you promote your business benefits them too.

Give copies to existing customers and encourage them to share them with friends and family. Create a "new customer" welcome package with copies of your book and instructions on how to give it away as a referral tool. These days, personal referrals are one of the most effective ways to get new business, and using your book as a referral tool is very smart.

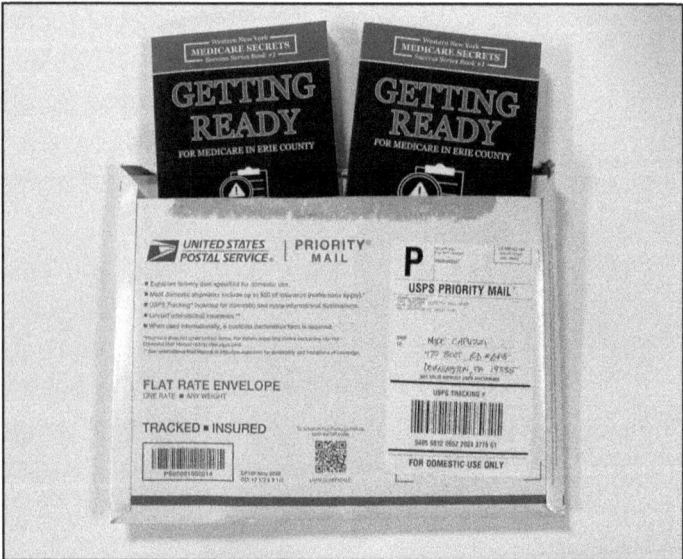

Two Books Package From Andrew Hibbard

GIVE YOUR BOOK AWAY TWO AT A TIME

This tactic is so simple and obvious that most authors don't often do it (myself included at times). If someone asks for a copy of your book, one smart way to extend its power is to send two copies and let your recipient know you have included a "bonus" copy of your book so that they can share with a friend or family member who could benefit from it.

When I do this, I am very explicit in my language as to why I included a bonus copy and what the primary recipient should do with it. For example, "*I am including a second copy of my book for you to give to a family member or friend who could use this valuable information.*"

In many cases, this allows your primary recipient to give away a valuable gift to one of their contacts (which is a good feeling to encourage).

For just the cost of a second book, you can generate goodwill, additional value, and word-of-mouth marketing within a network of people you may have never reached otherwise.

Dr. Ashley Lucas on The Mike Gallagher Show

GIVE YOUR BOOK AWAY
TO INFLUENTIAL PEOPLE

I dentifying the top influential people in your industry and niche and giving them a copy of your book can be a great way to generate buzz and exposure for it, especially if the person recommends and shares it with their audience.

The key to this tactic is to come from a place of adding value to the influencer's audience. Influential people get pitched all the time and your book and request will be no different unless you can add value to their efforts.

My client, Dr. Ashley Lucas, leveraged this tactic when she sent a copy of her book to Mike Gallagher, host of The Mike Gallagher Show (a top-rated podcast).

Mike had her on his show and discussed her book and this endorsement led to many of his listeners getting a copy of it.

My Podcast Interview Book Gift Site

GIVE YOUR BOOK AWAY WHEN YOU DO INTERVIEWS

Being interviewed by influential people, the media, and podcast hosts is a great way to share the message of your book and oftentimes, there is no cost other than your time.

The key is to find the right types of interviews where your target ideal reader is reading, listening, or watching. The next critical step is to get permission from the interviewer to share your book. Here is a simple system I have set up for myself and use frequently when I am a guest on others' podcasts.

During the interview, instead of sharing my website or social media profiles, I offer a valuable gift and direct people to a hidden page on my website that I only use for interviews. You can see what my current one looks like on the previous page.

This has a ton of value for listeners, but it also allows me to build my email database for future follow-up. An added benefit is that it allows me to know which podcast a listener heard me on.

PART 4

EVENT TACTICS

"My existing and prospective clients appreciate receiving my book as a gift. Showing your credibility through authorship is powerful and by focusing on giving it away (instead of trying to sell it), I have been amazed by the return on investment."

—Nick Guinn,
Intellectual Property Attorney

EVENT TACTICS

In this section I am going to focus on a variety of "event tactics." Events, both virtual and in-person, give you a variety of ways to get your book in front of your ideal readers.

As you read through this section, I challenge you to identify the event tactics you can and should start using immediately.

Nick Guinn at His Book Signing Event

GIVE YOUR BOOK AWAY AT A BOOK SIGNING EVENT

Now that you are a book author, it should come as no surprise that your audience will want autographed copies of your book! I will never forget the first time this happened to me. I thought the woman who was asking me was joking. Trust me, it will happen to you too!

One fun and unique way to get your book out there is to either host your own book signing event or be part of a larger event's book signing opportunity. This is a great way to create some buzz and photo opportunities.

My client and attorney, Nick Guinn, did this recently when he launched his new book and hosted a nice little event at a local winery that was also a client of his. This collaboration allowed Nick to feature his client's winery and bring a nice crowd together for good food and drink.

Nick also donated all book sales proceeds to a local non-profit that was featured at the book signing event.

JOIN US FOR

An Evening With The Authors

WEDNESDAY, JUNE 19, 2013, *from* 6–8 PM

AT THE MANHEIM TOWNSHIP PUBLIC LIBRARY
595 Granite Run Drive, Lancaster, PA 17601

Join us for an evening to discuss historic preservation issues and get answers to your questions about vexing older home care problems. Authors Chuck Groshong and Danielle Groshong-Keperling, of Historic Restorations, will present an overview of their recently released *"Preservation Primer, Volume #1: Avoid Common Mistakes that Cause Irreversible and Costly Damage to Your Historic Building's Architectural Integrity."*

Light refreshments will be served.

Hosted by the
CENTRAL PENNSYLVANIA PRESERVATION SOCIETY
Space is limited. Preregister to receive a complimentary copy of "The Primer" (a $24.95 value) at the event compliments of the Central PA Preservation Society.

RSVP BY JUNE 12, 2013 *by calling (717) 291-4688 or by visiting www.preservationprimer.com/CPPS*

"Evening with the Author" Example
From Danielle Keperling

GIVE YOUR BOOK AWAY AT AN EVENING WITH THE AUTHOR EVENT

This tactic is very similar to the previous one except that instead of promoting a book signing event, you are promoting *"A/An Morning/ Afternoon/Evening with the Author"* event.

This type of event has a different feel and purpose than a book signing event in that typically there is a presentation or even a book reading that goes along with it. Depending on your book's focus, this type of event could be ideal.

My friend, Danielle Keperling and her husband, published a short book a few years back on the topic of preserving historic homes and buildings. During the launch of the book, she worked with a local preservation society to host *An Evening with the Authors* event where they signed copies of their book, did a short presentation, and answered questions.

I also love the fact that they mentioned they would provide a free copy of their book ($24.95 value) when one pre-registered for the event. Very smart strategy!

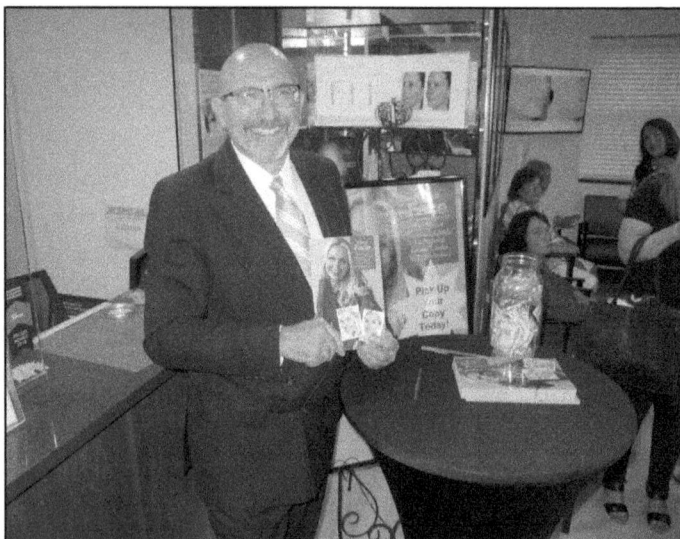

Dr. Eric Dohner's Book Launch Party

GIVE YOUR BOOK AWAY AT AN IN-PERSON BOOK LAUNCH EVENT

If you own a local business, hosting an in-person book launch event can be a fun, engaging and profitable endeavor. Your new book is a great *reason why* to host this type of an event for existing customers and new prospects. The key is giving yourself time to promote in your own media and in local media and then host a fun and informative event.

Dr. Eric Dohner, a vascular surgeon in New York, has held these types of parties for his various books with great success. He hosts a party with prizes, food, and drinks and an informational session based on the book he is debuting. Of course, he also does a book-signing session. These book launch parties result in valuable customer engagement and sales from both existing customers and prospects.

I interviewed Dr. Dohner on my podcast, and it's worth a listen to learn his strategy:

https://AuthorFactor.com/dr-eric-dohner

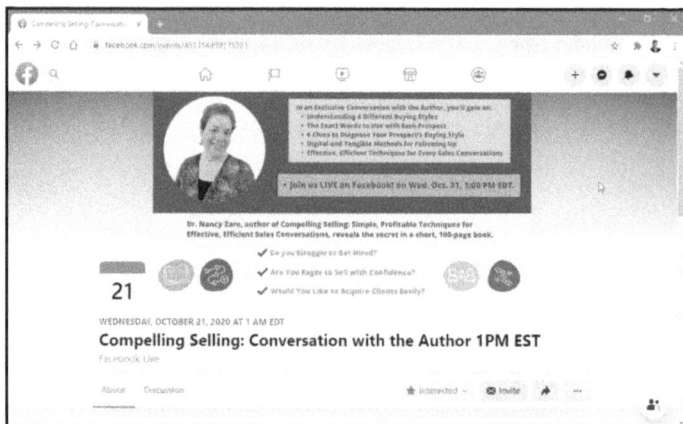

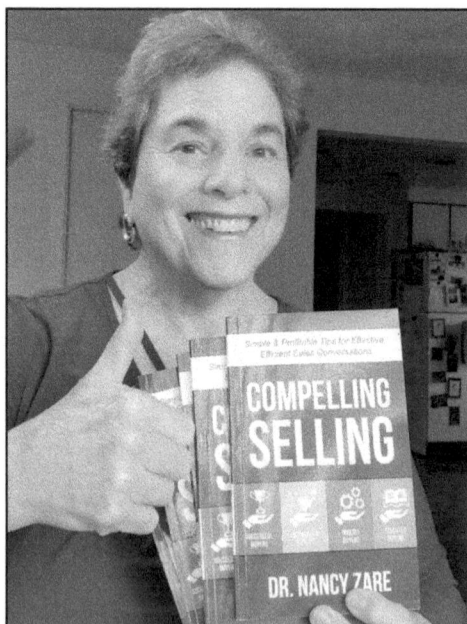

Dr. Nancy Zare's Virtual Launch Event

GIVE YOUR BOOK AWAY AT A VIRTUAL BOOK LAUNCH EVENT

Once your book is available, hosting a virtual book launch event is a smart way to share the news of its release. You can easily host such an event with Zoom, which is what my client, Dr. Nancy Zare, did with the launch of her book, *Compelling Selling*.

My personal preference is to create a simple presentation that aligns with my book's content to give attendees a taste of what the book is all about and why they want to grab a copy. You can either do this as the host of your own event or have someone else be the host and interview you. You can even have customers or clients as special guests for social proof that what you do works.

Regardless of the strategy you use, I highly suggest creating a limited-time special "launch offer" for your book and some related bonus gifts. Consider:

- Digital bonus gifts (eBooks, special reports, related videos, or trainings, etc.).

- Physical bonus gifts (products you sell, signed book copy, etc.).

Michelle Lank Smith's Event Exhibit

GIVE YOUR BOOK AWAY AT AN EVENT YOU ARE EXHIBITING AT

Many business owners are familiar with and have exhibited at various types of events and conferences. Being face-to-face with hundreds or thousands of potential prospects is a time-tested way for generating new business.

Using your book as a lead generation offer at events is a powerful way to differentiate yourself and your business. Instead of giving away candy, pens, or some other gift that will get eaten or thrown away, offer your book as "the thing" to get. Here is the strategy I suggest to clients, like Michelle Lank Smith, who exhibited at a local community fair:

- Create a big banner sign that promotes your free book offer.

- When attendees ask for a copy, have them fill out a three-question questionnaire and include their business card/contact info. This allows you to "grade" the lead after the event.

- Autograph the book as you give it to the attendee.

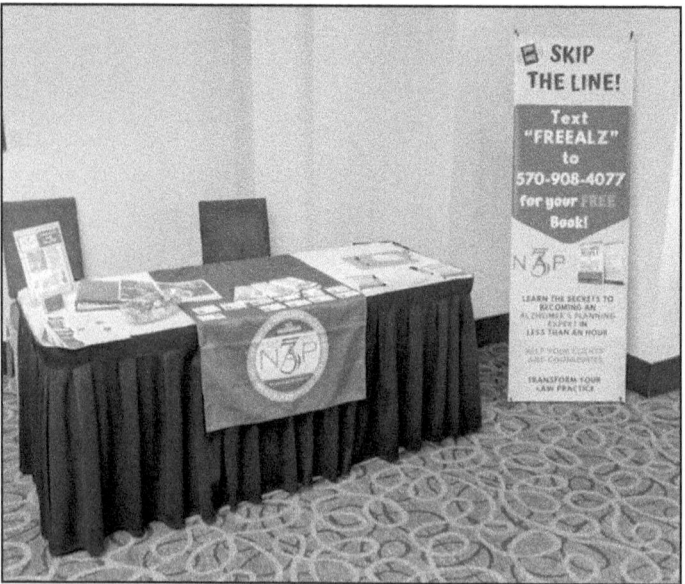

Julie Steinbacher Sharing Her Book at an Event

GIVE YOUR BOOK AWAY AT AN EVENT YOU ARE SPEAKING AT

Event hosts love to feature book authors as speakers at their events, and now that you are a book author, you have the opportunity to leverage this strategy to be a keynote or breakout session speaker at events. Finding such opportunities typically requires a dedicated strategy, but the more you and your book are out there (on podcasts, in articles, etc.), the better your chance for getting noticed and getting invitations to speak.

While this strategy may not be for everyone reading this, if the idea of being on stage and giving a presentation that showcases your expertise interests you, then I say go for it! You can craft your presentation around your book and then offer your book as a take-home resource.

You can give away or sell your book at the back of the room, or even allow the host to purchase copies to give away to attendees beforehand.

My Event Attendees Received a Copy of My Book

GIVE YOUR BOOK AWAY AT YOUR OWN EVENTS

If you host your own events, you have a great opportunity to either give away or sell your book to your attendees. A few years back I even went as far as creating a book that I used for specific monthly marketing events I hosted.

Here are a variety of ways you can use your book when it comes to your own events:

- As a pre-registration bonus gift.

- Include personalized autographed copies in an attendee welcome gift bag.

- As a bonus gift for doing something at the event (e.g., actively participating, buying something, making a donation, etc.).

- As a gift for bringing a guest.

- Allow attendees to take an extra copy or two to give to their friends.

PART 5

OFFLINE MEDIA TACTICS

> "*I am amazed at my results. Within 30 days of displaying my free book offer in a few local businesses where I know my prospective patients visit, I was able to get three new patients, each worth thousands of dollars to my practice .*"

> **—Dr. Kevin Flood**

OFFLINE MEDIA TACTICS

In this section I am going to focus on a variety of "offline media tactics." Offline media is any type of media that is not digital or online. Think "old-school" traditional print and broadcast media.

While there is no denying the cost, speed, and opportunities presented by online media, the smart author leverages offline media in addition to online media. There are tons of opportunities to get your book in front of the right people by using a few offline media tactics.

As you read through this section, I challenge you to identify the offline media tactics you can and should start using immediately.

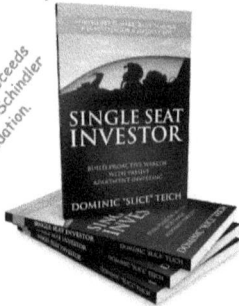

Dom Teich Featuring His Book In His Newsletter

GIVE YOUR BOOK AWAY VIA YOUR PRINT NEWSLETTER

If you publish a printed newsletter, you have the ideal media to announce your book and keep it in front of your audience over the long term. Here are a few ways you can use in your newsletter:

- Announcement article.
- Reader testimonials.
- Reader success stories.
- Highlights from your book.
- Reader photos.
- Book graphics.
- Special book offers.
- Free book "advertisement."

My client, Dominic Teich, used his monthly printed newsletter to announce the debut of his first book, *Single Seat Investor.*

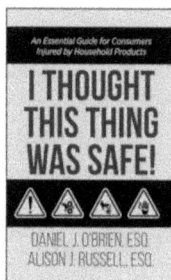

Dan O'Brien and Alison Russell's Advertorial

GIVE YOUR BOOK AWAY
VIA AN ADVERTORIAL

Advertorials are a unique type of print advertise-ment and an effective strategy to market your book. Advertorials have been used for decades and are designed to look like articles in publications.

These information-rich ads are typically used for lead generation marketing where you are trying to get a certain reader to raise his or her hand and request your book. Advertorials follow direct-response mar-keting copywriting guidelines, including:

- An attention-grabbing headline.
- Who you are and why you wrote your book.
- Who your book is for.
- What they will get from it after reading it.
- A book photo or image.
- Clear call-to-action with ways to respond.

If you want more information about advertorials, visit https://MikeCapuzzi.com, type "advertorials" in the search bar and you will find a number of related articles.

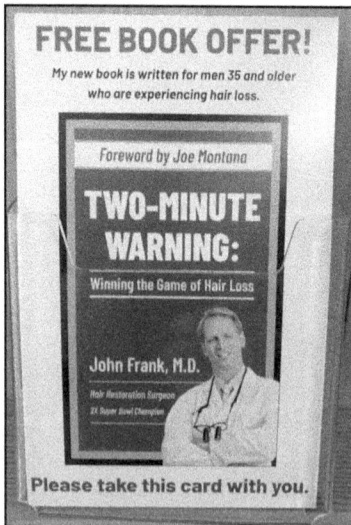

Strategic Partner Display Examples

GIVE YOUR BOOK AWAY IN STRATEGIC PARTNERS' BUSINESSES

This is one of the smartest and most effective ways for many types of authors to get their book in front of the right prospects, especially what I call "Main Street Authors." These local business owners/ authors can leverage this powerful strategy quite effectively (and profitably) as my clients have.

The strategy is to give strategic business partners either copies of your book or a book promo card to display in their place of business, and offer a free copy to their customers/clients/patients/students. The key here is to make sure your strategic partner(s) have your targeted ideal book readers flowing through their businesses. If you can find a few like this, you have big opportunities.

My client, Dr. Kevin Flood, worked with several local business partners, and because he was a holistic dentist, displaying his "mercury-free dentistry" book in health food stores, yoga studios, chiropractor offices, and similar businesses enabled him to attract several new patients within just a few weeks.

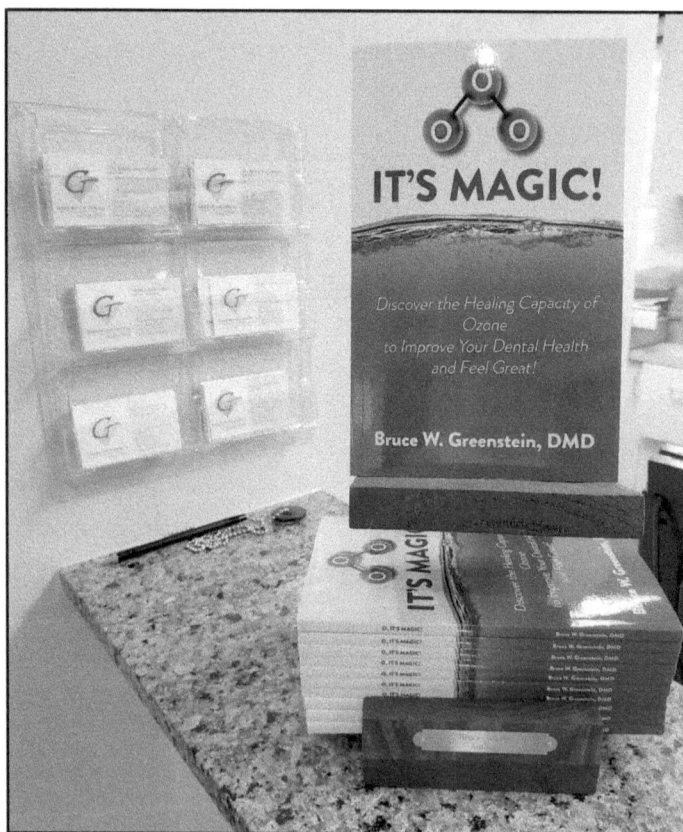

Dr. Bruce Greenstein's In-Office Display

GIVE YOUR BOOK AWAY IN YOUR BUSINESS

Featuring your book strategically in your store, office, or place of business (assuming prospects and customers visit you) is a smart way to promote it. Encourage visitors to take a free copy for themselves and for friends and family who could benefit from it. Consider displaying your book in these locations:

- At your "checkout" location.

- In your waiting room or lobby.

- In your consultation room.

- In your showroom.

One of the gifts we give our publishing clients, once their book is completed, is a unique type of personalized book display that allows them to show off their book in their business or office. You can see Dr. Bruce Greenstein's example here.

I do not suggest you sell your book, though some authors do. My suggestion is to offer free copies, or if you want some skin in the game, ask for a donation for a non-profit that you support.

Caroline Capuzzi's Book Featured in Local Store

GIVE YOUR BOOK AWAY
TO LOCAL STORES

If you are still fortunate enough to have a local bookstore (new or used books) or other retail stores where your ideal reader can be found, you should contact the owner and offer him or her the opportunity to sell (or give away) your book with no cost to them (e.g., you give them the copies and allow them to sell and keep all the proceeds).

Chances are your book will not have an International Standard Book Number (ISBN), so they will simply place it on something like a "Local Authors" display table.

There really is no good reason why they would not do this for you, especially if you are a fellow, local business owner and you are not asking them to pay for the copies. My daughter did this with a local store that prominently featured her "dog rescue stories" book in a special "Rescue" in-store display.

Is Poor Sleep Affecting You or Your Family?

My FREE New Book Gives You Helpful and Insightful
Tips and Strategies to Sleep Better!

SLEEP BETTER

JERRY LeCOMPTE

I published this book for the person who is seeking helpful and concise information about achieving better sleep. It is my hope it will provide useful information to you if:

- You or your partner is sleeping poorly and not getting the type of restful sleep you deserve.

- You are confused about all the different types of mattress solutions available to you.

- You are looking for a local and trusted expert to guide you to sleeping better!

It is my sincerest intention and commitment to provide valuable information to help Naples residents achieve the best sleep of their lives!

REQUEST YOUR FREE COPY TODAY!

CALL (239) 597-5333 TO GET YOUR FREE COPY!

Dear Friend,

If you or someone you know is being affected by poor sleep, I want you to know about a new book I just published. *Sleep Better* is written for individuals and couples who are dealing with sleep issues and are looking for expert advice and guidance on the most important things to sleep better.

My book is designed to be read in about an hour or two and provides clear and simple advice, guidance and tips.

For a limited time, you can get a copy of it absolutely free by calling (239) 597-5333 or emailing us at info@naplesmattress.com and letting us know where to send it. Or you can visit one of my stores.

- Naples Mattress (North) 13560 Tamiami Trail N Naples, FL 34110

- Naples Mattress (East) 11566 Tamiami Trail E Naples, FL 34113

- Cape Coral Mattress 791 Del Prado Blvd N Cape Coral, Fl 33909

There is no obligation and I look forward to sharing this important information with you.

Jerry LeCompte

Sleep Better Is For You If:

- You believe in the power of guidance from an experienced and local expert.

- You are confused by all the hype and mis-information surrounding buying the right mattress.

- You understand your situation is unique, and your path may be different than those of your friends and loved ones.

GET YOUR FREE COPY TODAY!

Jerry LeCompte
Naples Mattress/Cape Coral Mattress
13560 Tamiami Trail N
Naples, FL 34110

A Free Book Postcard From Jerry LeCompte

GIVE YOUR BOOK AWAY VIA A POSTCARD

The simple lead generation postcard that features the announcement and availability of your free book is a time-tested strategy to get interested people to request a copy of it. This strategy can be used by both the local business owner or the business owner who serves a larger audience.

Unlike Every Door Direct Mail, these types of postcards are sent to a known list and can be personalized. They are also relatively inexpensive to print and mail.

I wrote a short marketing analysis and featured several real-world examples of using a lead generation postcard focused on a free book. Check it out on my blog at:

https://MikeCapuzzi.com/book-promotion-postcard

An EDDM Example From Jeff Giagnocavo

GIVE YOUR BOOK AWAY VIA EVERY DOOR DIRECT MAIL

Every Door Direct Mail (EDDM) is a special service offered by the United States Postal Service, and it enables you to do highly targeted direct mail at big cost-savings.

You can literally choose specific neighborhoods or business areas based on carrier routes and a variety of other demographics. It is a cost-effective way to get a lead generation message in front of a lot of people. Just be aware that EDDM is not personalized to the recipient and everyone in the targeted area will get your mailer.

If you are a local business owner, EDDM is a great way to announce your free book to your local community with a simple, postcard-style mailer. For more information about EDDM, visit USPS.com and search on Every Door Direct Mail. If you work with a business that does your mailings, they should have no problem creating an EDDM mailer for your free book.

Print Ad Example From Tiffany O'Connell

GIVE YOUR BOOK AWAY VIA LOCAL PRINT MEDIA

In many communities, local print publications are still alive and thriving. In addition to traditional local newspapers, there are free community papers, glossy "neighbor" magazines, and a variety of sports- and health-focused publications.

These local publications offer you a proven way to get your free book offer out into your community, and if you can combine it with having a featured article written about you (like lawyer Tiffany O'Connell did), that is a powerful one-two, lead generation punch.

Another powerful opportunity is offering to write a regular column focused on the topic of your expertise. Years ago, I did this for our local newspaper and was able to write several months of columns focused on small-business marketing (thereby getting my name and expertise out in our community for months). Do your due diligence and you might uncover an excellent publication your ideal readers are reading.

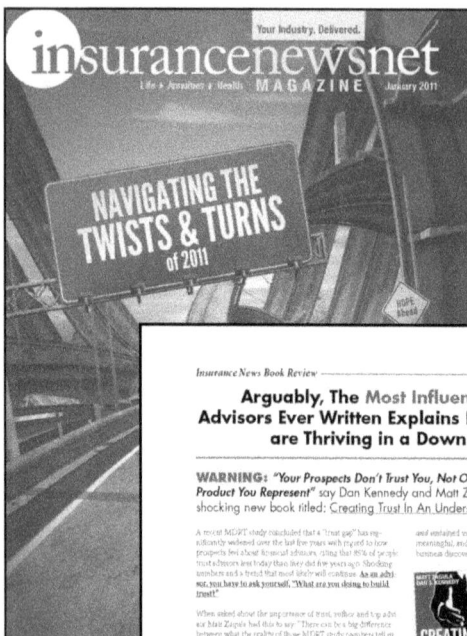

Ad Example From Matt Zagula and Dan Kennedy

GIVE YOUR BOOK AWAY VIA INDUSTRY PUBLICATIONS

If your free book is written for other business owners in a specific business niche or industry, consider creating a lead generation advertisement in publications and magazines that serve the focused audience. Done right, this type of offer can be effective.

Matt Zagula and Dan Kennedy hit a home run with this strategy when they promoted their book, *Creating Trust*, in a magazine their ideal prospects read. In this particular ad, they did several notable things you should consider, including:

- Making the ad look like an advertorial.
- An attention-grabbing headline.
- A book image.
- Compelling copy that is designed to motivate the reader to take action.
- Clear and simple directions on two different ways to get a free copy of the book.

Infomercial with Book Offer From Jeff Giagnocavo

GIVE YOUR BOOK AWAY VIA LOCAL BROADCAST MEDIA

If you use local radio and TV to advertise your business, creating a free book "spot" is another effective way to get your book offer in front of an appropriate audience.

Personally, I would only encourage this specific strategy if you are currently using local radio or TV advertising or have experience using it. There are a lot of moving parts (and costs) associated with doing this type of traditional advertising, but depending on your targeted audience, it can be quite effective.

The key thing to remember with using TV or radio is to make your call-to-action very simple and memorable. A phone number, QR code, and/or URL that can be easily remembered is best.

Check out how Jeff Giagnocavo and the team at Gardner's Mattress & More did this by producing an informercial:

https://LessSnoreMoreCuddle.com/videos

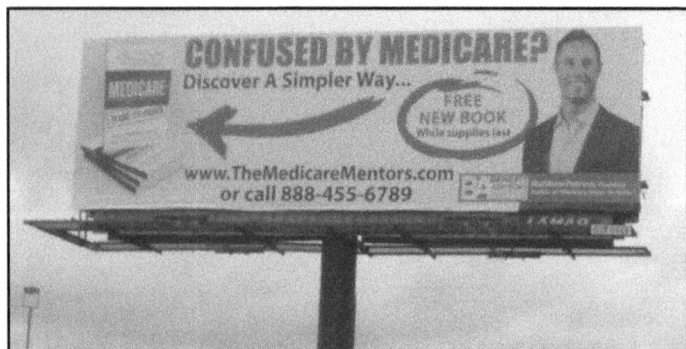

Roadside Billboard Ads Featuring a Free Book

GIVE YOUR BOOK AWAY VIA OTHER LOCAL MEDIA

M ost local business owners never publish a real book, which automatically differentiates those that do from their competition. It also allows them to make unique and different offers that stand out from the "same old, same old" ads featured in most local media.

Here are a few unique media options local business owners can use to feature their book offer. Just keep in mind your targeted reader and what media will get your book in front of them.

- Door & mailbox hangers.
- Roadside billboards (traditional and digital).
- Local social media groups.
- Sports field banners.
- Local influencers.
- Diner menus.
- School publications.
- Local magazines.

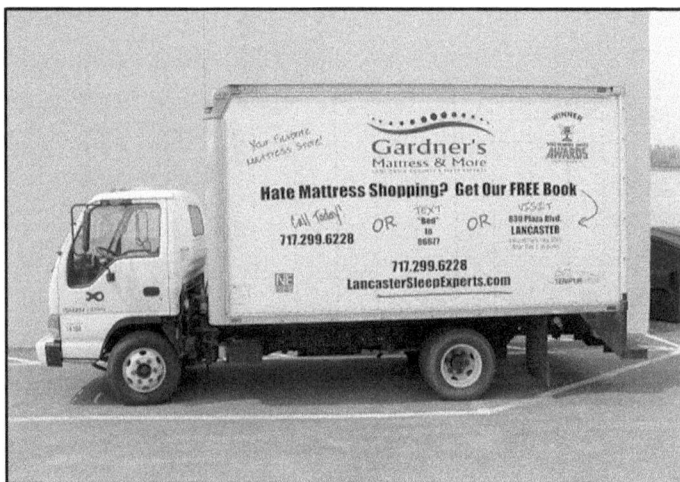

Book Offer on Delivery Truck From Jeff Giagnocavo

GIVE YOUR BOOK AWAY VIA VEHICLE MARKETING

If your business uses vehicles that have signage or a wrap to promote your business, adding the offer to get your free book is just another way to get it in front of potential leads and does not cost you any additional money (other than creating the sign or wrap)!

My longtime client, Jeff Giagnocavo, who is a mattress retailer in Lancaster, PA, was the first business owner I know who featured his free book on the side of his delivery truck.

If you study the photo on the previous page, you will see that Jeff is following many smart copywriting techniques, including:

- Interesting headline.
- Clear call-to-action.
- Multiple ways to get the book (e.g., QR code, phone number, URL).

PART 6

ONLINE MEDIA TACTICS

"Giving away my free book on my website has resulted in over $40,000 in new member revenues in just the first few months of using it as part of my free book marketing strategy."

—Ashley Lucas, PhD.
Founder of PHD Weight Loss

ONLINE MEDIA TACTICS

In this section I am going to focus on a variety of "online media tactics." Online media is any type of media that is digital or online.

As you read through this section, I challenge you to identify the online media tactics you can and should start using immediately.

Jeff Arnold Offering His Book On One of His Sites

GIVE YOUR BOOK AWAY VIA YOUR ONLINE MEDIA

Chances are, you are using a variety of your own online media channels to advertise, market, and promote your business. This list includes media like:

- Your blog.
- Your email marketing.
- Your website.
- Your podcast.
- Text messaging.

You should leverage all of these once your book is published to let the various people who follow you know about it and how to get it. The more you can consistently and persistently do this, the better your results will be.

My client, Jeff Arnold, promoted his new book, *Money Secrets*, in a variety of websites he owns, including *The Arizona 100*.

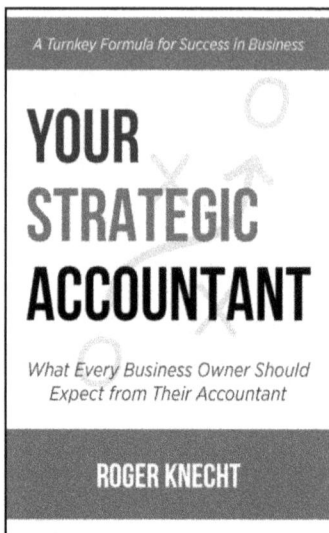

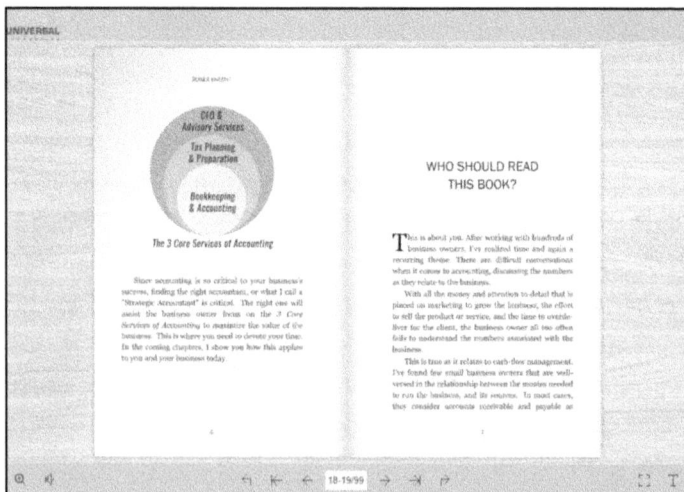

A "Flip" Book Example From Roger Knecht

GIVE YOUR BOOK AWAY AS A FLIP BOOK

My favorite (and recommended) type of free book is the traditional paperback variety. Maybe it's because I grew up reading printed books, but I feel like there is nothing like handing someone a copy of your printed book and even signing it for them. This is kind of hard to do with a digital book.

However, digital books have their place, and besides the familiar PDF, Kindle™, Nook™ and other eBook formats, there is one type of digital format I like to use, which we also create for clients.

I call it a "Flip" book, named after the software used to create it. This software allows you to convert a static PDF book into an interactive, media-rich eBook that is easily shareable on a website or by email. If you check out their "Showcase" on their website, you will get ideas for your own Flip book.

Want to see one I created for my business? Visit:

https://BiteSizedBooks.com/authors

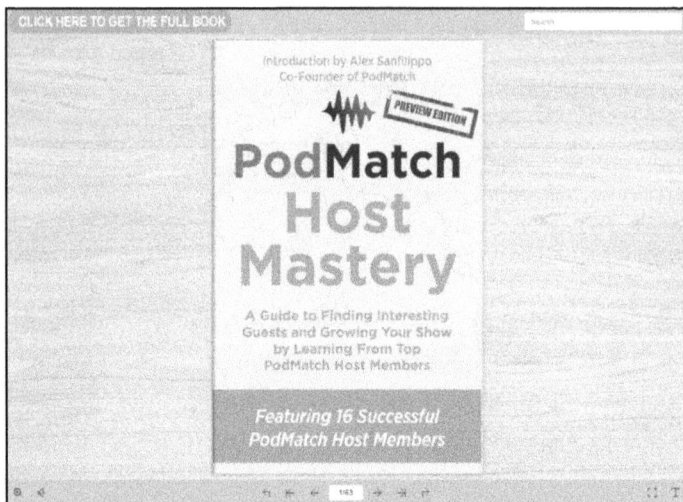

GET THE FULL EDITION OF THIS BOOK HERE...

You can get the full edition of *PodMatch Host Mastery* by visiting:

https://PodMatchBooks.com

Preview Book Example From Alex Sanfilippo

GIVE YOUR BOOK AWAY VIA A PREVIEW COPY

If you are against giving away your book (or circumstances do not allow you to give it away), there is one simple tactic that allows you to still offer a "free book." It's what I call the "Preview Copy" or "Preview Edition" version of your book.

The Preview Copy is an abbreviated version of your book which strategically contains the first few chapters of your book along with a clear call-to-action instructing readers how to get the full version of the book. Make sure you clearly identify that the book is a preview version right on the cover.

The way I instruct my clients to leverage the Preview Copy is to create a Flip version of it and give that away. Throughout it you should include several repeated calls-to-action (CTA) to get the whole book.

On the previous page, you can see the Preview Edition (in Flip format) of Alex Sanfilippo's book. We put a button on the Flip book and included several CTA pages inside the shortened version.

~ October 13, 2019 ~

Nigel Moore -- Package Price Profit

I had a great chat with my old friend Nigel Moore from Australia about his new book, **Package Price Profit**.

(You can buy it on Amazon in paperback or Kindle edition.)

This book is a great overview of pricing and bundling options in the IT service industry. I particularly love his analogy about so-called All You Can Eat: Everything at the buffet is included. If you want us to make a special dish for you, that's not included!

Of course Nigel is also the founder of the Tech Tribe – www.thetechtribe.com. So we chatted about that a bit.

The official book site is www.packagepriceprofit.com.

▶ 0:00 / 32:28 ━━━━━━━━━━━━━━━━━━━━━━━━━━━━━━━━ ◀)) ⋮

Nigel Moore Promoting His Book on a Podcast

GIVE YOUR BOOK AWAY ON OTHERS' PODCASTS

Podcasts are quickly becoming a super effective way to share your book, and one of the best book - marketing tips is to be a guest on other people's podcasts. Here's how to make this happen:

- Create a list of ideal podcasts that are relevant to the topic of your book. You can do this by searching podcast directories (iTunes, Google Podcasts, Spotify, etc.) or do a Google search.

- Send an interview "pitch" to the host and focus on how your expertise and book are important and will help his/her listeners.

- Send an Author One-Sheet or digital media kit that showcases your expertise and book.

I have used this tactic many times to get on podcasts and in front of an audience that I would not have done so otherwise. If this idea interests you, check out the book *PodMatch Guest Mastery*.

https://PodMatchBooks.com

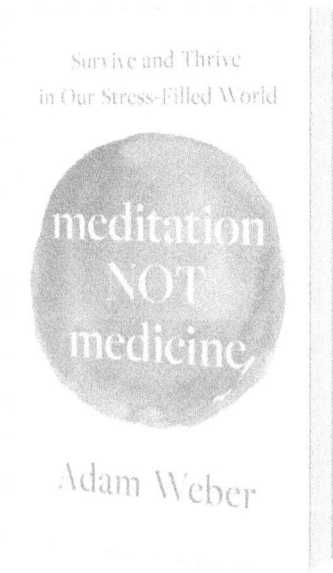

Adam Weber's Podcast and Book

GIVE YOUR BOOK AWAY ON YOUR PODCAST

If you are the host of a podcast, just like other "you own it" media, you have a unique opportunity to leverage to promote and give away your book. If you are not yet a podcast host, you might want to consider creating a show around the theme of your book (like my client, Adam Weber, did with *Meditation Not Medicine*).

Here are some ways to promote your book on your podcast:

- In the show's introduction.
- As a "sponsored" ad in the middle of your episodes.
- As a listener giveaway.
- As part of a listener contest.
- On your show's website.
- In show notes.

If you have an interest in starting your own book-themed podcast, reach out to me and I will be happy to hear your ideas and give you some feedback.

Free Book Offer on Website From Dr. Ashley Lucas

GIVE YOUR BOOK AWAY ON YOUR MAIN WEBSITE

Whereas creating a book-specific website is optional, offering your book on your main website is critical. You want to feature it so all website visitors see it and request a copy. Here are a few strategies to consider for website promotion:

- Offer to send a free print copy in exchange for full contact information.

- Offer to send a free print copy and visitor only pays for shipping.

- Offer an online Flip version in exchange for name and email.

- Offer a Preview Edition in exchange for name and email.

The big idea here is to make sure your book(s) are easy to find and easy to get on your website(s). If you have multiple books, consider creating a page where they are all featured, like I do on my website:

https://MikeCapuzzi.com/author

Book-Specific Website Example From Jeff Shamus

GIVE YOUR BOOK AWAY VIA A BOOK-SPECIFIC WEBSITE

Creating a dedicated and focused book-specific website is an effective way to promote your free book offer. A book-specific website can be as simple as a one-page WordPress site that uses an easy-to-remember URL and eye-catching graphics (like I did with https://MarketingWithFreeBooks.com). This would be an ideal URL to use in all the various media you are promoting the offer in.

You can enhance this website by adding a video of you talking about the book, a few SEO-rich articles on it (so Google can find it), and even some "hidden" pages that can be referenced inside the book. You can also create a Preview Edition of your book and use that as an opt-in download. My suggestion is to offer to send the printed book at no cost or "free but pay for shipping."

By the way, if you are wondering what the difference is between a book website versus a book funnel, a funnel has a choreographed series of sequential "steps" a visitor goes through, whereas a website is just one step.

Book Funnel Example From Stephanie Boris, Esq.

GIVE YOUR BOOK AWAY
VIA A BOOK FUNNEL

Chances are you have seen a free book offer on social media, which is the 21st century version of the classic free book offer. These offers typically are the starting point of what is known as a *free book funnel*.

A free book funnel is typically a strategic, online combination of media and offers designed to attract ideal readers, get them to say "yes" to the initial free book offer, and then present a series of upsells and even down-sells to the new customer. The goal is to turn your paid advertising into a profitable effort right from the get-go.

Some authors just offer a free downloadable book, but more sophisticated funnels offer the printed version for free, but the customer has to pay for shipping.

I've developed something I call *The Perfect Book Funnel*, which is my own formula for creating an effective book funnel strategy for most non-fiction book authors. If you want to learn more, reach out to me.

Gardner's Mattress | Sleep Better | Free Book ⓘ

[Ad] www.gardnersmattressandmore.com

Our book, Sleep Better, gives you helpful tips & strategies to get a better night's sleep. Make sure to request your Free copy of our book before you buy a mattress anywhere 120 day Comfort Guarantee. Types: Double Sided.

Natural mattress guide

Download a free guide

📞 Call (717) 299-6228

Google Ad Example From Jeff Giagnocavo

GIVE YOUR BOOK AWAY
VIA GOOGLE ADS

According to the market research company Forrester 93% of online experiences begin with a search. An important part of leveraging this reality is Pay Per Click (PPC) advertising, which is dominated by Google Ads. I will not pretend to be a Google Ads expert, because I am not, but I do know those people exist and are able to help business owners tap into the power of Google Ads.

Mattress retailer, Jeff Giagnocavo, works with one such expert, and they have recently tested a number of Ads campaigns. Their real-world results show that ads featuring a free book get more clicks than traditional mattress-focused ads.

Jeff has tested a number of recent Ads campaigns, and those ads featuring his free book offer and free buyers' guides have converted into more leads and customers for his business than campaigns focused on mattresses.

Facebook Ad Examples From Julie Steinbacher

GIVE YOUR BOOK AWAY VIA SOCIAL MEDIA ADS

Depending on your business and ideal customer, running online lead generation campaigns for your free book may be a great fit. My Facebook feed is filled with free book offers, and this strategy can work regardless if you have a local business or a global business.

Potential social media includes:

- Facebook
- Twitter
- Pinterest
- Instagram
- LinkedIn
- YouTube
- Amazon

Unless you have the budget, I would recommend sticking with the online media you have experience with and offering your free book there.

Dr. Doug Lucas' YouTube Channel

GIVE YOUR BOOK AWAY VIA YOUR YOUTUBE CHANNEL

R ecently, I was having a consulting call with Dr. Doug Lucas, an orthopedic surgeon who I am working with to publish a short, helpful book about osteoporosis. Doug is a successful medical doctor and business owner who does a lot of marketing. During our meeting, he shared with me that his current top two organic traffic sources for his business are:

1. Podcast guesting.

2. His YouTube channel.

I specifically asked him about his YouTube channel, since I have heard from other successful business owners about they how create weekly (or even daily) short YouTube videos and generate massive amounts of organic traffic for their various efforts (including their book).

If you have the desire and ability to quickly and easily produce your own videos, I would highly encourage you to research this more. And make sure you check out the latest A.I. offerings to make this easier and faster.

MIKE CAPUZZI

Publisher Author Podcast Other Interviews About Q

Announcing The 100-Page Book (An Amazon Best Seller)

By Mike Capuzzi | 1 💬

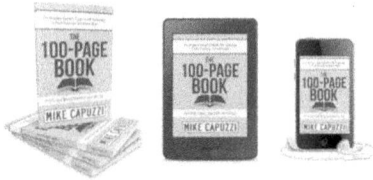

My latest short, helpful book (shook™), *The 100-Page Book*, is now available on Amazon as a print book, Kindle book and audio book, and as of today's date, it is the #1 bestseller in several business related categories for both the Kindle and print version (special thanks to all who grabbed a copy and those friends who helped me spread the word!).

But first a warning, this book is not for everyone. *The 100-Page Book* is not focused on convincing you to write a book or showing you how to make money *selling* books. Instead, this is all about how to create a strategic sales tool for your business, by self-publishing a book.

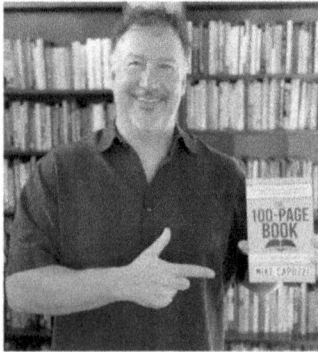

▶ BUY NOW!

Online Article Example From Me

GIVE YOUR BOOK AWAY VIA ONLINE ARTICLES

If you have a blog or you write articles for other blogs, writing a blog post announcing the release of your book, and embedding related topical keywords people are searching on, will help your book be found during online searches.

How fast and effective this is depends on how popular your blog is in the "eyes" of Google and the other search engines, but regardless, I still encourage clients to write at least one blog article about their book. At a minimum, you can email the post to your list.

I also recommend inserting several images of you and your book and even reader photos to make it more engaging. Just make sure you name these graphic files the same name as your book to help with Google image searches (e.g., 100-page-book-1.jpg).

Finally, make sure you link all your book-related posts to the main way a reader can get your book (e.g., your book funnel, your book website, Amazon, etc.).

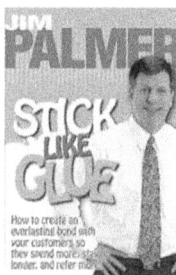

Stick Like Glue - How to Create an Everlasting
Bond with Your Customers
★★★★☆ 26

Kindle Edition
$0^{00} $9.99

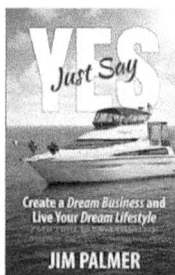

Just Say Yes: Create Your Dream Business and
Live Your Dream Lifestyle
★★★★☆ 51

Kindle Edition
$0^{00} $9.99

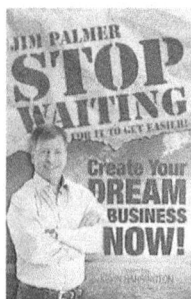

Stop Waiting For it to Get Easier: Create Your
Dream Business Now
★★★★☆ 96

Kindle Edition
$0^{00} $5.99

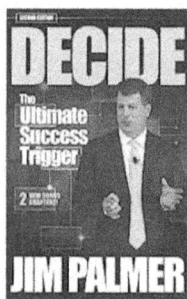

DECIDE - The Ultimate Success Trigger
★★★★☆ 49

Kindle Edition
$0^{00} $6.99

Other formats: Paperback

Free Kindle Book Offers From Jim Palmer

GIVE YOUR BOOK AWAY AS A "PERMAFREE" KINDLE BOOK

I must confess, I have never used this strategy, but I have seen other authors, including my long-time friend and multi-book author, Jim Palmer, leverage the tactic of a "*permafree*" (permanently free) Kindle book on Amazon. In Jim's case, he has several free Kindle books and at the time of me writing this chapter, over 35,000 Kindle versions of his books have been downloaded.

There are many eyeballs that could eventually turn into valuable book reviews, opt-ins to your email list, and future clients.

If you Google "permafree books on Amazon" you will find several videos, articles, and even books on the topic which will show you how to get Amazon to set your Kindle book pricing to free.

If you are unable or do not want to have your Kindle versions for free, you have a few other opportunities to leverage the power of Amazon. Check out the next two tactics.

$0.99 Kindle Book From Dr. Ashley Lucas

GIVE YOUR BOOK AWAY AS AN ALMOST FREE KINDLE BOOK

When you set up your print and Kindle books on Amazon, you have the opportunity to set your own pricing, though there will be a minimum required by Amazon based on your book specifics. Obviously, most book authors price their books higher because the royalties Amazon pays are their main income source from their books.

I don't do this because strategic authors like me understand the power and reach of Amazon (and that it is essentially a huge search engine for information-seekers and buyers). Instead of pricing our books so we make a few dollars every time one is sold, we price our books at the bare Amazon-set minimum or slightly above it to make it easy for people to say yes and buy. For many Kindle books this can be as low as $0.99.

The key to making this profitable for you is to ensure your book has specific and strategic opportunities for readers to connect, opt-in, and buy from you.

Promotion & Advertising on Amazon KDP

GIVE YOUR BOOK AWAY VIA A FREE BOOK DEAL ON AMAZON

As an Amazon KDP (Kindle Direct Publishing) author, you can take advantage of a few different types of advertising and promotional opportunities, including running a Kindle Countdown Deal or a Free Book Promotion for up to five days of each 90-day enrollment period.

You can run this promotion for a consecutive five days or break it up over the course of three months.

While you won't receive royalties on your book during this period, it may be worth it. You'll increase the odds of ranking on Amazon's Top 100 Free list, which is great exposure for any author.

You will also get a bump in book reviews and if you have embedded calls-to-action in your book, you will see a bump in those too.

> *"I didn't write the book to make money by selling the book. I wrote the book as a "leave behind" when I meet with prospects so they have a better understanding of what it's like to work with me."*

—Walter Crosby,
Founder of Helix Sales Development

CONGRATULATIONS!

Congratulations! You made it to the end and more importantly, I hope you are now ready to create your own Smart Author Toolkit and leverage several of the various "free book marketing" tactics I shared.

If you want to learn more about how I help business owners, entrepreneurs, and corporate leaders publish and use short, helpful books with a distinct "direct response marketing" flavor, please keep reading.

PART 7

BITE SIZED BOOKS

"*Mike's expertise and guidance were invaluable in navigating the complex publishing industry, and he went above and beyond to help me achieve my publishing goals. Throughout the entire process, Mike was responsive, communicative, and always willing to answer any questions I had. He took the time to understand my vision for the book and helped me craft it into a finished product that exceeded my expectations.*"

**—Jeff Arnold,
Founder of RIGHTSURE**

WHO RELIES ON ME?

Choosing the right publishing partner for you and your business can be a stressful and overwhelming decision. You don't want to make costly and glaring mistakes, and you want to ensure your time, effort and money investments are going to pay off.

The bottom line is working with a publishing partner should give you the *peace of mind* you deserve. While your final decision will be based on a gut feeling, I do believe you can never have enough information, which is why I wrote *The Magic of Free Books* for you. It would be my honor to serve you like all the other business owners I have been able to help to date. To give you a better picture of the types of people I am best able to serve, here is a brief overview of some of those who rely on me for their short, helpful book publishing.

Savvy professional service providers, including lawyers, insurance agents, tax professionals, and financial advisors.

WHY?

Because these types of business owners offer complicated, in-depth solutions to a variety of issues, and they need to streamline their message into a concise, easy-to-understand format, like a short, helpful book. Instead of getting bogged down in heavy details, these business owners need to convey authority and trust in meaningful ways. My proven shook publishing system does exactly this by offering just the right balance of information, guidance, and next-step directions.

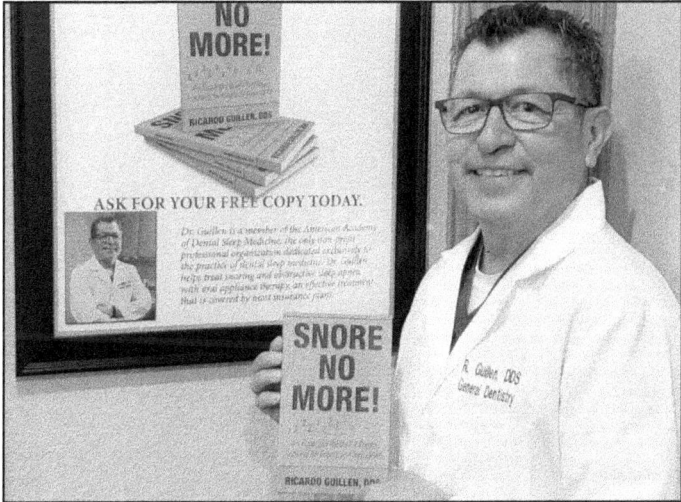

Forward-thinking healthcare professionals, including dentists, physicians, chiropractors, surgeons, and therapists.

WHY?

Because there is nothing like combining impressive academic credentials, established experience, and the power of being a book author to create exciting new opportunities for you and your patients. Left on their own author journey, these types of business owners can often get bogged down in the scientific minutiae that confuses readers. My clients rely on my vision of the "bigger picture" to keep them and their shooks on point and on target.

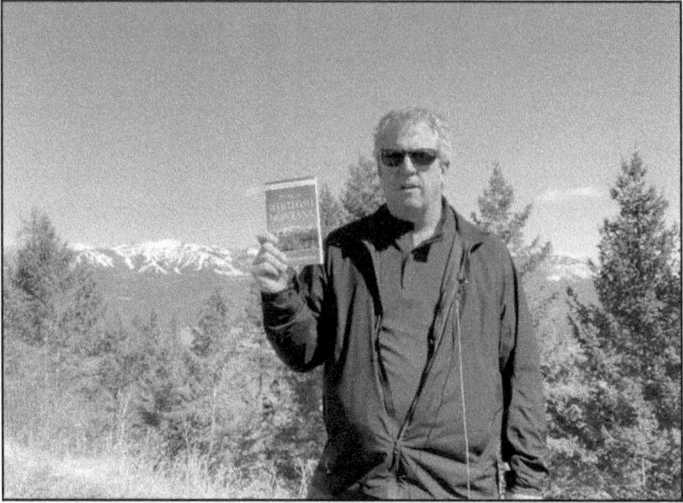

Innovative high-ticket or luxury product/
service providers, including retailers
and real estate professionals.

WHY?

Because high-end and luxury-oriented consumers expect their product and service providers to be different, unique, and known as expert authorities. The more affluent your clientele, the more critical it is for you to correctly position yourself and your offerings and be the author of the type of book that immediately raises your status and celebrity and creates a powerful, magnetic effect that draws these affluent clients *towards* you.

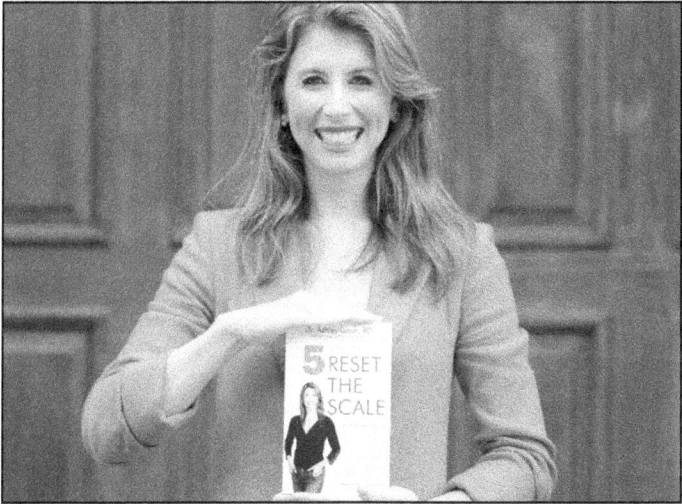

Coaches and consultants determined to stand out, be different, and be recognized as a valued subject matter expert.

WHY?

Because the business world is full of coaches and consultants who have little to show why anybody should do business with them and why their vision, methodologies, and systems matter. When I work with coaches and consultants, I spend time helping them uncover what truly makes them special and their unique gifts to be able to help others. Crafting this as the foundation of a shook is one of the most powerful things any coach/consultant can do.

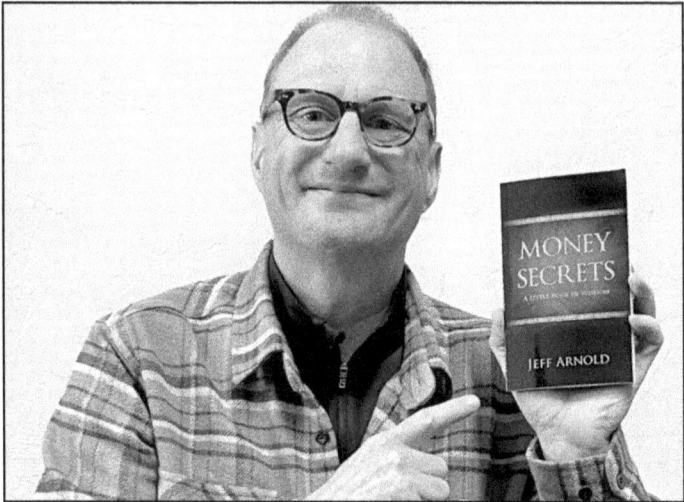

Time-strapped corporate executives and leaders who have an important message to share with their team or the world.

WHY?

Because corporate executives and leaders do not have the luxury of blindly wasting their time and energy on writing the wrong book. It is critical for these men and women to develop the right "shook hook" and then deliver on that promise. These leaders and executives rely on my skills to make sure we have the ideal shook plan and then rely on my team to take their vision, thoughts, and ideas to create the perfect shook.

THE BITE SIZED BOOKS
AUTHOR PROGRAM

I hope by now you're convinced that a shook, created to be used as the centerpiece of a *free book* marketing strategy, is a must-have and valuable asset for you and your business. You can spend money on things like brochures, logos, and videos, but nothing has the staying power of a real book.

I published my first book in 2007 and helped my first client publish his first book in 2008. For several subsequent years, I helped clients publish a variety of different short books. And in early 2019, I formalized my publishing service and created Bite Sized Books.

Bite Sized Books is unique because we are a nonfiction, short book publishing company that only serves business owners, entrepreneurs, and corporate leaders and we do so for these three reasons:

1. **We only publish short books that can be read in about an hour or two** (typically less than 15,000 words) and are written and designed to be a marketing and sales asset. Our shooks follow a classic "direct response marketing" formula.

2. **Our business owners/authors are not focused on trying to make money by selling their books**, but instead, will leverage the time-tested "*free book*" marketing strategy and give their book to as many qualified readers as possible.

3. **I am your primary point of contact, and you will only work directly with me**. I do not shlep you off to an assistant or inexperienced newbie. Instead, you are working with a successful and experienced fellow business owner who has been helping clients improve their marketing since 1998. This gives you the peace of mind you deserve when working with a publishing partner.

Straight-Forward, Cost-Effective Options for Publishing Your Book

The reality is, there are a bunch of places where you can make costly mistakes when publishing a book for your business. Considerable time should be given to the content, structure, goals, and promotion of your shook, and this cannot be done in an hour or two, or even in a day. At least, not in my opinion.

My *Bite Sized Books Author Program* offers you straightforward, simple, and cost-effective publishing options, and if you have read this far, I am sure one is ideal for you.

Our publishing options include everything you need to go from idea to printed book. Regardless of the option you choose, know that when you work with me, in whatever capacity, you benefit from my decades of experience, making sure you don't stall, trip, or fumble.

When we work together, you will get the best of me working for you, and you get an all-inclusive and personalized opportunity to get your shook done right and done fast. We will have scheduled meetings and you will have direct access to me as I guide you step-by-step. Before you know it, you will be a short, helpful book author and have a professionally published shook working for you and your business.

What You See Is What You Get

I believe in being honest, straightforward, and transparent, which is why I put all the details for our Bite Sized Books Author Program right on our website.

https://BiteSizedBooks.com/program

The Next Step

If you would like to have a "mini mastermind" session with me to discuss your short, helpful book idea, all you need to do is schedule your Shook Strategy Session. There's absolutely no fee, no obligation, no risk, and nothing to lose. Here's what to do:

1. Visit https://BiteSizedBooks.com/program.

2. Review my Bite Sized Books Author Program options and pricing to see which program may be right for you and your business. Please make sure you do this before our meeting.

3. Click the Shook Strategy Session button and follow the prompts to schedule either a Zoom meeting or phone call with me.

ABOUT MIKE CAPUZZI

Mike is a publisher, an Amazon #1 best-selling author, and coach for business owners looking to uniquely position themselves, differentiate their business, and attract new customers easily by authoring and publishing a short, helpful book.

Throughout his two-plus decades as a marketing strategist, Mike's innovative use of *high impact marketing* has consistently surpassed the expectations and outcomes of traditional marketing concepts and business strategies for his clients.

His expertise has led him to be a guest speaker on the stages and podcasts of some of the world's most foremost experts on books and marketing, including Dan Kennedy and Bill Glazer. To date, Mike has helped thousands of business owners around the world create more effective and profitable marketing.

Mike is the inventor of the successful library of direct-response graphics known as CopyDoodles®. CopyDoodles are hand-drawn graphic files that enable anybody to literally drag and drop attention-grabbing enhancements to their offline and online marketing materials. Tens of thousands of business owners, marketers, and copywriters have benefited from the use of CopyDoodles (check out https:// CopyDoodles.com).

In 2019, Mike launched Bite Sized Books, a new publishing venture founded on his proven formula for creating short, helpful books (known as shooks) for business owners. Shooks are ideal for business owners who are looking to increase their level of authority while also providing helpful information in bite sized books.

Mike is also the host of *The Author Factor Podcast* where he interviews business owners, entrepreneurs, corporate leaders, and book experts on real-world, proven ways to leverage a book to position themselves and promote their business.

To learn more about Mike's opportunities, visit https://MikeCapuzzi.com, and if you're looking for a content-rich, unique speaker for your in-person or virtual event, or podcast, contact Mike for his speaker kit.

THE AUTHOR FACTOR
PODCAST

The Author Factor Podcast is an interview-style podcast with host, Mike Capuzzi, and business owners, entrepreneurs, corporate leaders, and guest experts who have successfully authored, published and leveraged a book in their business to differentiate themselves and attract more ideal customers, clients, patients, or students.

Ranked globally in the top 5% of all podcasts by Listen Notes, each weekly episode shares insights, tips, and ideas on how others use their book to create the *ultimate competitive advantage*. Listen at

https://TheAuthorFactor.com

Or your favorite podcast directory! And if you are already a published author, consider joining me as a guest. Details on the website.

FREE READER RESOURCES!

As an exclusive and special gift for readers of this book, I have created a private, reader-only page where you can:

- Download valuable resources, including the shook building blocks, bonus trainings, and more.
- Get quick access links to recommended book writing and design resources.
- Get quick access links to recommended book printing resources.
- Get quick access links to recommended book marketing resources.

VISIT:

https://BiteSizedBooks.com/resources